CONCILIUM

Religion in the Eighties

e Seabury Press
multiplied and/or
any other manner
jmegen (Holland)
ss Inc., New York

h EH2 2LQ

ork, N.Y. 10017

o.: 80 54392

Sons Ltd., Edinburgh

and Canada) £27·00 posta
stage and handling included.
) Subscription distribution in
ison Avenue, Suite 1217, Ne

SEABURY PRESS
New York

CONCILIUM

CONCILIUM

Religion in the Eighties

CONCILIUM

Concilium 150 (10/1981): Moral Theology

CHRISTIAN ETHICS: UNIFORMITY, UNIVERSALITY, PLURALISM

Edited by
Jacques Pohier
and
Dietmar Mieth

English Language Editor
Marcus Lefébure

T. & T. CLARK LTD.
Edinburgh

THE SEABURY PRESS
New York

December 1981
T. & T. Clark Ltd., 36 George Street, Edinburgh EH2 2LQ
ISBN: 0 567 30030 7

The Seabury Press, 815 Second Avenue, New York, N.Y. 10017
ISBN: 0 8164 2350 4

Library of Congress Catalog Card No.: 80 54392

Printed in Scotland by William Blackwood & Sons Ltd., Edinburgh

Concilium: Monthly except July and August.
Subscriptions 1981: All countries (except U.S.A. and Canada) £27·00 postage and handling included; U.S.A. and Canada $64.00 postage and handling included. (Second class postage licence 541-530 at New York, N.Y.) Subscription distribution in U.S. by Expediters of the Printed Word Ltd., 527 Madison Avenue, Suite 1217, New York, N.Y. 10022.

CONTENTS

Part II
Philosophical Problems about Universality and Particularity

Part III
Theological Solutions to the Problem of Uniformity, Universality and Pluralism

Editorial

THE VARIOUS human sciences—history, cultural anthropology, sociology, psychology, etc.—all agree that there are many moralities. The history of religions—whether the history of different religions or that of the same religion—also attests this pluralism.

Within Catholicism the problem of ethical pluralism arises in a way that is at once more complex and more conflict-ridden. On the one hand, the Roman Catholic Church has the conviction that it is possessed of the morality that is in closest conformity to Scripture and Tradition (even if it acknowledges that it is very far from living up to its ideal); it even goes as far as sometimes giving the impression that in its opinion the same Scripture and Tradition in the last analysis legitimates only this form of morality. From this point of view it inclines more towards being morally monolithic rather than pluralistic.

On the other hand, ever since it declared itself open to ecumenism it has felt obliged to recognise the genuinely Christian character of the moralities of the other churches.[1] What is more, it has come to grips from within itself with the difficult problem of finding itself implanted in the post-Christian forms of western culture or in non-western or non-Mediterranean cultures—an implantation the failures and limitations of which are often tied to Christianity's incapacity to evangelise and vivify these other cultures and other ethical values (as distinct from just suppressing them and replacing them by a western-Christian culture and its ethics). And finally, at least so far as the West goes, the benefits of ethical pluralism are demonstrated (and sometimes even put in practice) by the secular and democratic conception of society. Even if the Church wishes to keep its proper distance from the world, it cannot remain insensible to a current the theoretical and practical results of which deserve respect.

The Catholic Church therefore finds itself in a situation of conflict and difficulty in the matter of ethical pluralism. On the one hand, everything that presses it to affirm the oneness of the faith, the Church, ecclesial power, etc., also tends towards an affirmation of the oneness of Christian morality. Under this pressure people can even maintain that this Christian morality should be uniform across the diversity of times and places, so that 'catholicity' is here interpreted in terms of uniformity. On the other hand, strong internal and external forces push in the direction of an acknowledgment and furtherance of a certain ethical pluralism.

This is why there has for some time now been an abundant literature in Catholic theology about this question of ethical pluralism and its possibility in Catholicism—and the very differences in orientation, not to say the occasional contradictions, reflect just how far Catholicism is divided on this issue. This present issue of *Concilium* does not, of course, purport to resolve this difficult problem. It does, however, set out to tackle it on the basis of a particular option which itself constitutes one of the essential contributions of this issue.

The fact is that most theological writing on this subject poses the problem in terms of the *possibility* of ethical pluralism in Christianity: the foundations of Christian faith are investigated and the question is asked whether these foundations warrant such a pluralism, and, if so, under what conditions.

The line we take in this issue is diametrically opposed to this: we take the view that moral pluralism is a *fact* within Christianity, a reality that has obtained for twenty centuries, from the time of the primitive communities which predated the composition of the texts of the New Testament until our own day. We think that this fact is not in the first place the result (although it could sometimes be that too) of imperfection, approximation, deviation or errors on the part of individuals or communities, but that it is a normal occurrence in Christianity, and a beneficial one at that, so that the 'catholicity' of the Church consists not in a uniformity of morals but in communication and communion—across time as well as across space—between local communities or individuals who have been led to work out different moralities but who can recognise each other to be sharers of a faith in the same Lord.

We therefore think that it is necessary to look at the problem in a completely different way and to start not from principles which might justify or condemn ethical pluralism but from facts which show that ethical pluralism has always existed in Christianity, and even within communities and theories said to be 'orthodox', that is to say, acknowledged to be in accordance with the faith by the community of believers.

That is why the whole of the first part of this issue is meant to establish the sheer fact of moral pluralism within 'orthodox' Christianity. Two articles illustrate this pluralism in the past: the first example consists in the diversity of attitudes prevalent in the primitive Church towards an abidingly central problem in Christian ethics, that of concupiscence (in all the theological senses of this term) (*Murphy*), whilst the second example is provided by the profound change represented by the transition in the middle ages from an 'intellectualist' to a 'voluntarist' model of morality (*Ernst*). Two further articles give examples of this pluralism in contemporary Christianity: one shows the differences between a morality inspired by the social doctrine of the Church and one inspired by the theology of liberation (*Boff*). And we know that this is no merely bookish problem, because a Latin American bishop, Mgr Proaño did not hesitate to declare in this very journal (*Concilium* 130, 10/1979, at p. 63) that the Catholic Church in Latin America was split into two from top to bottom on this issue, as on so many others. The other article deals with what are still today the sociological and theological differences between 'Catholic' and 'Protestant' moralities that are experienced in a confessionally mixed country such as Switzerland (*Fuchs*).

Finally we thought it fitting to conclude this first part of the issue on moral pluralism as a datum by giving two examples of situations where Christianity finds or has found itself at grips with a culture completely alien to the western one, and where the possible future of Christianity in these cultures seems to us to depend closely on whether or not Christianity will be able to do justice to the essential ethical values of the culture in question. The case of the wisdom of China seemed an obvious choice (*Ching*) in view of the fact that the difficulty Catholicism has made to make itself relevant to Chinese culture has for four centuries been one of the most serious failures of the 'catholicity' of Christianity. The case of African family tradition is an equally burning topic (*Odi Assamoi*) because we know what difficulties the young churches of Africa experience in the meeting between traditional Catholic morality and the tradition of African family life.

These six articles constitute the first half of this issue, and, as we have already indicated, are meant to make clear the sheer *fact* of ethical pluralism within Christianity itself. In this connection we take the liberty of underlining the fact that these six articles are written by six authors coming from six very different countries and four continents: an American from the United States of America, an East German, a Brazilian, a Swiss Protestant, a woman religious of Chinese race, and an African mother of a family. In an attempt to establish the fact of pluralism, the cultural pluralism of the authors is no mere editorial whim, it is an epistemological necessity.

It is at this stage, and only at this stage, that theoretical reflection on ethical pluralism comes in. This reflection has been pushed so far by philosophers that it seemed indispensable to reflect on what, since Kant, for example, the criterion of the universality of the moral judgment could be in the face of the diversity of historical moralities (*Quelquejeu*) and on the plurality of moralities could mean in the perspective of the dialectical theories of Hegel and Marx and in terms of the challenge they present to our societies today (*Dussel*).

The four themes tackled in the theological articles that comprise the last part of this issue are the classical theological themes that arise out of a reflection on ethical pluralism: unity and plurality in the morality of the New Testament (*Blank*), the *magisterium* as a guarantor of unity (*McCormick*); nature or reason as a criterion of the universality of morality (*Korff*); moral pluralism and unity of the Church (*Komonchak*). At the same time we think that the reader will be able to see for him- or herself that each of these articles brings new and constructive insights to topics that may well be classical in themselves. And it is part of our thinking that these reflections should contribute simultaneously to the necessary pluralism of ethics and to the necessary unity of the Church.

The fact is that this problem of ethical pluralism is often tackled in a polemical context which is easy to understand—and perhaps even to excuse—but which it is also absolutely necessary to transcend. Those who favour ethical pluralism often deploy this latter as a weapon of war against the central authority of the universal Church, the uniformism and monolithic character of which they denounce; contrariwise, the holders of the central authority of the Church are tempted to suspect every move in the direction of ethical pluralism of being an attempt to divide the Church or relativise the faith, and this possibly out of a concern to preserve their power but certainly to preserve the values of unity and truth which they want to serve and promote. In such a case they just talk without hearing each other.

We, however, aim in this issue of *Concilium* to serve both the values of pluralism and the values of unity; we want it to be a constructive contribution to the realisation of both these sets of values and to the working out of their co-existence. That is why we are very glad that, for example, precisely the two articles that are devoted to the Church (*McCormick* and *Komonchak*) both carry a pressing appeal to Christian men and women to take constructive responsibility *both* for the elaboration of a particular morality appropriate to their local church *and* for the elaboration of the unity in the faith to be promoted between the local churches within the universal Church, including the *magisterium*, in respect of which every single member of the community of the faithful, men and women, have an active responsibility, as *McCormick* emphasises.

We should like to add two other remarks, which are of a different order, but which seem of capital importance to us. The reason why we wanted to look at the problem from a different angle than the usual one and to start from the *fact* of pluralism is not that pluralism is, in our opinion, the actual starting-point within the history of societies, individuals and their religions. On the contrary, as *Quelquejeu* stresses, the starting-point is historically the absolutisation of *its* morality by each group and individual by identifying it with morality *as such*. Pluralism is a hard-won conquest, involving the mutual confrontation of individuals and their moralities and the ensuing questioning of their moralities by each individual group. Wanting true ethical pluralism is not merely a matter of noting, with the pleasant scepticism of the cultured man, that the diversity of moralities reflects the shimmering richness of the human condition; no, it means getting involved in an individual and collective struggle to take possession and put down the roots of the foundations of one's own uniqueness as a human being (and believer) and of the foundations of the universality of one's call to be a human being (and a believer). In this sense one could say that true ethical pluralism is eschatological in nature: it constitutes an axis of history rather than a reality that can easily be realised within history itself. And, like every eschatological reality, it is what is at the source of, and what is at stake in, a difficult struggle to change the face of this world and to bring a new world to birth therefrom.

Our second concluding remark does not concern the traps inherent in too idealistic and abstract a conception of pluralism, as our first one did, but rather the traps inherent in what is also too idealistic and abstract a conception of universality. Alike in its religious as in its philosophical forms, the idea of the universality of ethics was born around the shores of the Mediterranean and in Europe. It is true that its theoreticians did their utmost to think it through in its most theoretical and universal form. But we are more conscious than people were in the past that even the most abstract and universalist ideas are not independent of the historic, cultural, political and socio-economic conditions in which they arose. We can, moreover, no longer ignore the fact that theories about the universality of ethics, whether philosophic or religious, were worked out in (and by) countries which were economically and culturally masters of the world, or at least considered themselves to be so. The authors of these theories were certainly unaware (and innocent) of this correlation. The distrust and protests emanating from other cultures should, however, alert us to the fact that this European idea of the universality of ethics can be a front for an imperialism which would like to impose ideas of universality.[2]

Here again, as in the case of pluralism, true universality is not a starting-point that is easily accessible even to a very high culture or to a thinker of genius: it is the result of a conquest and hard individual and collective work. Like true pluralism it too is perhaps eschatological in nature, it too is more like an axis applicable to history rather than a reality easily realisable within history itself. And like every eschatological reality it is at the source of, and what is at stake in, a difficult struggle to change the face of the world and to bring a new world to birth therefrom.

Should the Church not be a privileged agent in this double struggle? It would seem to be part of its specific calling. But this would seem to require, as we have already observed above, that its 'catholicity' should not be the result of a monolithic uniformity, but the fruit of communication and communion—across time as well as across space—between local communities which have been and will be led to work out the particular ethics that are appropriate to their local church but which can recognise each other to be sharers in a faith in the same Lord.

JACQUES POHIER
DIETMAR MIETH

Translated by Iain McGonagle

Notes

1. Reasons of space in a single issue devoted to this theme prevent us from making a study—very interesting as that would have been—of the moralities professed and practised by non-orthodox groups and individuals.

2. It so happens that we pen these lines just at the time when something is happening in the Catholic Church that illustrates this unconscious and involuntary imperialism of the western churches very neatly. Before the opening of the 42nd Eucharistic International Congress held at Lourdes from 16-23 July 1981, an important theological symposium gathered together 150 participants in Toulouse from 13-15 July, on the theme: 'Sharing the Eucharist and Responsibility'. The French conference of bishops had had a 'message to the world' prepared by three of its experts dealing with the way in which the Eucharist is a source and principle of sharing. The delegates from the Third World opposed the delegates from the western countries and threw out the first and second version of this message, on the ground that it was too dependent on western conceptions of economics and sharing, let alone of the Eucharist and the faith. Specially worthy of attention are the contributions made by Pierette Attouo, an economist from the Ivory Coast, Fr Marcello de Carvalho Azevedo, a Brazilian Jesuit, and Fr Dis Amalortavadass, an Indian theologian, who levelled this objection not only against the report submitted to the symposium but against the official Eucharistic prayers of the Roman Catholic Church.

PART I

The Fact of Ethical Pluralism in Christianity Down the Centuries and Today

Francis Murphy

Concupiscence (Epithumia): A Key to Moral Pluralism in the Early Church

IN A peculiar historical lapse, Pope Paul VI at the close of the 1974 Roman Synod of Bishops declared that Peter and Paul had not given the Christian message an alien vesture by adapting it to the Jewish, Roman or Greek mentality. Theologies based on cultures or continents, he said, could be dangerous. The fact, of course, is that Peter and Paul and their successors did adapt the message preached by Christ in Aramaic, within a Judaic context, to the culture of the Greco-Roman world in which they found themselves. The primitive Church quickly developed diverse theologies based precisely on the cultural and continental differences between Alexandria, Rome and Antioch. To this day there is a fundamental contrast between the scholasticised doctrinal explanations of the gospel in the western tradition and the mystical theologies of the Oriental churches.

1. THE MORAL TEACHING OF THE PRIMITIVE CHURCH: ITS RELATIONSHIP TO THE JEWISH TRADITION AND GREEK CULTURE

One area in which this diversity reveals itself in cultural adaptation is in the moral sphere. It is now generally recognised that the primitive Church made a clear distinction between the *kerygma* or apostolic preaching and the *didache* or moral instruction contained in the initiation of the catechumens called the *catechesis*. Recent research has clarified the elements of the gospel proclamation that characterised the preaching of Paul and the New Testament witnesses. As heralds of very important news, the Christian preachers confronted their audience with the life and deeds of Christ in brief form, demonstrating that in Christ's conflicts, sufferings, death and resurrection, the divinely guided history of Israel had reached its climax. God himself had intervened in history to inaugurate his kingdom upon earth. The listener was now face to face with his Lord manifest in Christ's earthly *basileia* or kingdom which was the new Christian community or Church. The convert had only to accept Christ's invitation to embark on a new life wherein, through God's mercy, he would be unburdened of past delinquencies and enjoy a new and close intimacy with God in Christ Jesus, dead and risen from the dead. Once inserted into the new community, the catechumens were given instruction in moral principles and sanctifying conduct that were essential to the Christian way of life.[1]

This order of presenting the new Christian fact—first the *kerygma*, then the *didache* or moral teaching projected on an eschatological background—seems to have been characteristic of all the primitive Christian preaching. As such it was an outgrowth of the Jewish tradition. For both the Decalogue and the grand structure of the Law or Torah began with a statement of divine fact: 'I am the Lord your God . . .' (Exod. 20:2) supported by events portraying God's providence and backed by moral requirements or commandments.

The Christian moral teaching thus inherited from its Judaic origins a dynamic sense of God's wisdom which permeated creation and sanctified the one who devoted himself to the cultivation of God's Law or the Torah. In the Law was embedded the way of wisdom (*hokmah*) to which the devout Jew was led by the *derek tebunot* or divine insight into the right conduct of life. The rabbis had developed this doctrine in a moral and spiritual sense, insisting that the *shekinah* or divine presence only inhabited the heart of the humble, giving him wisdom. Thus evil inclinations could be overcome by the contemplation of the Torah which made the wise man gentle, kind and pious.[2]

St Paul applied this rabbinic way of wisdom to Christ, the 'power and wisdom of God' (1 Cor. 1:24). As the body of Christ, the Church is the way of wisdom, the final realisation of God's plan of salvation. H. Jaeger points out that this identification of Christ and Wisdom gave rise to two different but mutually dependent traditions in the early Church. In the later New Testament documents and the post-apostolic fathers the rabbinic, homiletic tradition prevailed. Wisdom was the achievement of holiness accomplished through the acceptance of Christ as Lord. With the later, second-century apologists, on the other hand, Christ is gradually identified with Wisdom in an attempt to demonstrate his divinity.

It is here that the Hellenic concept of *sophia* or wisdom formally enters the Christian theological development. The Septuagint translation of the Hebraic *hokmah* by *sophia* had been no accident. For in the old Greek tradition, sophia is more a virtue than a philosophical concept. It is used of one who 'practised what he preached'. And in later usage, it retained the notion of both superior knowledge and right conduct. Plato speaks of the wise man who 'becomes like God . . . by being just and holy' (*Theaitetos* 1761); and Plotinus speaks of wisdom as 'the life of the soul illumined from within' (*Enneads* V. 8. 4). In both Cicero (*Tusc.* V. 36, 195) and Virgil (*Georg.* 2, 490) *sapientia* is used in this sense of virtue.

There is a striking similarity between the moral thunderings of the ancient Jewish prophets (e.g., Isa. 2:12-17) and the ethical injunctions of Hesiod (*Works and Days*), Solon (*frag.* 36f.) and other early Greek thinkers. This fact, particularly in relation to the teaching of Plato and Socrates did not escape the notice of the early Christian churchmen beginning with Justin Martyr and Clement of Alexandria. They were influenced primarily by the Jewish sage, Philo of Alexandria (20 B.C. to A.D. 50) who had made a strenuous effort to bridge the Hebrew and Hellenic cultures. But the infiltration of Hellenic elements into the Judaic thought patterns had taken place much earlier. It is witnessed to by the Sapiential literature of the Old Testament. Thus while generally speaking there was a fundamental difference between the basic ideology of the pagan moralists, particularly the Stoics, and the Judeo-Christian doctrine, the technique of teaching, and most of the actual practices were all but identical.

The early Christian instruction exhibits many characteristics of the Greek culture in which it was propagated. Nor is this a strange phenomenon, for the itinerant Platonic, Cynic, Stoic and Epicurean philosophers preached a way of life that was radically identical. It was aimed at the practice of virtue whose goal was self-mastery. Its objective was to teach the individual to obtain full control of the passions and base emotional drives in order to achieve contemplation of the good with the Platonists; or with the Stoics, to arrive at what was just and proper (*honesta*) on the way to *autarxia* (self-mastery) and finally *apatheia*.

The later pagan philosophers from Plutarch and Cicero to Seneca and Marcus Aurelius, reflecting in good part Aristotle's *Nichomachean Ethics*, cultivated a self-contained, non-religious, logically coherent system of ethics based on the nature of man, and on a rational analysis of his reaction to daily experience. Recognising his inner self as fundamentally reasonable, man desired to direct his activities in an orderly fashion by mastering his passions and emotions, eliminating vice, and freeing himself from preoccupations with the baser interests of life.

Both Plato and Aristotle had developed the ethical teaching of Greek philosophy on the premise that the wise man was capable of controlling his inner drives by the practice of self control. In so doing, they distinguished between man's rational, irascible and concupiscible appetites. This became the common practice of the moral philosophers. It was taken over by the Church fathers once they began to give a reasonable explanation of their inculcation of ethical values. In general, however, the earlier churchmen made no attempt to analyse the nature of virtue as a human experience or endeavour; nor did they extinguish between intellectual and moral virtues. All formed an integrated pattern of the good life and, where the conclusions of right reason had been codified in law (*nomos*) obedience to the law was considered virtuous.[3]

2. CONCUPISCENCE (EPITHUMIA) ACCORDING TO THE GREEK MORALISTS

In the philosophic literature from Plato to the Neoplatonists, considerable attention was given to the psychological elements involved in man's evil tendencies. The effort was, however, greatly affected by a preoccupation with a world of good and evil spirits who had an intimate effect on human thought and conduct. In Homer, the most prevalent of man's wayward tendencies, *epithumia* or concupiscence had a neutral meaning. It was a desire or inner tendency towards some satisfaction. However, as the classic Greek ethic was dedicated to the achievement of moderation in human conduct, the Homeric man felt the need of subjecting his passionate feelings to control, although he attributed their origins to divine influence (*Iliad* 3, 139). With Pythagoras, Democritus describes unchecked sense-desire as folly which interferes with man's peace of mind (*ataraxia*) and destroys his self-possession (*autarchia*). Platonic dualism separated the body from the soul ontologically and divided the properties of the psyche into three parts: rational, irascible and concupiscible. Concupiscence (*epithumia*) was thus the movement within the lower parts of the soul that was outside the control of reason (*Repub.* IV. 335B-442A). For the later Aristotle, concupiscence is an irrational function of the sense (animal) appetite that is to be distinguished from rational desire lodged in the will (*Nich. Ethics* 1102a). The Stoics considered concupiscence as an irrational appetite in the soul, proceeding from a mistaken judgment in favour of a false or apparent good. Together with fear, lust, and sadness, concupiscence was one of the four affections which had to be rooted out through the practice of self-control for the achievement of peace of mind (Seneca, *Epist.* 116, 1). The later Stoics frequently identified concupiscence with lust. The Neoplatonists, pursuing a dualist concept of the soul imprisoned in the body, likewise insisted on ascesis as the annihilation of natural, corporeal tendencies, particularly of sexual desires (Porphyry, *Abst.* 4, 20). While the Stoics considered legitimate sexual activity justifiable, but not necessary (Epictetus, *Epist.* 3, 127), the Neoplatonists favoured absolute continence (Porphyry, *Ibid.* 1, 41). Most influential in patristic thought was the doctrine common to Hellenistic religious circles that postulated a trifold division in man's nature. Between the flesh (*sarks*) and the spirit (*Pneuma*) intervened the *psyche* (volitional faculty) which, while satisfying man's necessary corporeal desires, had to free man's spirit from inordinate appetites or concupiscence.[4]

In the Old Testament, man is considered a simple unity, hence the source of his evil-doing was traced to an evil heart (*cor malignum*) rebelling against God's Law. Later Jewish thought describes concupiscence as an internal movement whence arises disobedience to God's will. The rabbinic literature speaks of the *jeser hara* (internal evil movements) that can only be overcome by God's help. Despite the story of the fall in *Genesis* (3:7-11) no speculation on the connection between concupiscence and original sin is to be found in the Old Testament. Philo, in an amalgam of Greek dualism, the Stoic four affections, and rabbinic thought, traces concupiscence to unreasonable desires which can be brought under control by ascesis aided by man's contemplation of God's Law.[5]

3. CONCUPISCENCE IN THE NEW TESTAMENT AND ACCORDING TO THE GREEK FATHERS

In the development of its moral awareness that characterised the early Church, the analysis of concupiscence had its foundation in doctrines concerning original sin and the temptational powers of the devil as he was portrayed in the Scriptures. The first approaches to this aspect of concupiscence are to be found in the apocryphal literature of both the Old and the New Testaments. In the Qumran texts, besides an insistence on the influence of evil spirits, a connection is made between the body (*basar*) and sinfulness (*awel*). The older Jewish Apochryfa trace man's moral corruption to the union of the sons of God, and later, the demons, with the daughters of men (*Gen.* 6:1-6; *Henoch* 6-9). The later Apochryfa speak of an hereditary moral weakness that has its origin in an evil heart which is accompanied by a physical weakness implanted in Eve by the devil (*Apoc. of Moses*), a carnally centred concupiscence (II *Apoc. of Baruch*), and an inclination to evil that pre-existed the fall (IV Esdras).

In St Paul concupiscence is viewed in relation to man's salvation history (Rom. 5:12-21). It is an inner movement resulting from the effects of Adam's sin; but it is not identical with original sin. Paul contrasts *sarks* (flesh) and *pneuma* (spirit) (Rom. 7:4-6) but he does not mean simply a war between the flesh and the spirit (Gal. 5:17). *Sarks* is for Paul the godless, unredeemed state of man in contrast to the man who is spiritual, redeemed in Christ from the powers of Satan (Gal. 5:19-25). Concupiscence is present even in those regenerated through sanctifying grace; it is experienced as a lack, a potential source of sin connected with man's moral and religious relationships (Rom. 6:6; 7:3). It has an intimate bearing on death (Rom. 8:6). Finally, Paul stresses the 'powers of evil' which utilise the tendency of the flesh towards sin (Gal. 5:16-20) and puts the blame for sinfulness not so much on carnal infirmities as upon the rejection of God through the acceptance of the lawless realm of evil (*anomia*: Rom. 5:19; 7:25).

In James, concupiscence is the source of temptation (4:1-3) which destroys the love of God and leads to death (1:12-15); and in 1 Peter, there is a reference to carnal desires which war against the soul. Finally in 1 John, the things of the world constitute the concupiscence of the flesh, the concupiscence of the eyes, and the pride of life. They militate against the divine will, annihilating man's love of God (2:1-17).[6]

A valiant attempt to analyse the nature of concupiscence is made by Irenaeus who retains the Platonic dualism in its popular Greek formulation of spirit (*pneuma*), soul (*psyche*) and body (*plasma*) with the opposition between the appeal of the divine Word (*Logos*) through revelation and earthly attractions. He sees concupiscence as a sensual weakness; but in contrast to docetists and gnostic doctrines, while insisting on its corporeal origin, he maintains that concupiscence is possible only because of prior pride and disobedience in the soul. Despite the realism of his description of the complicity between pride and gross desires that constitute 'sensual wisdom' he is an optimist who sees man as a child being gradually educated by God for union with the Word (*Adv. haer.* 2, 26, 1; 4, 12, 5).[7]

For the Alexandrian fathers generally (Clement, Origen) concupiscence, while natural to the body, but susceptible of satanic stimulation, is a blocking-off of the true *gnosis* or knowledge leading to the contemplation of God. This Greek synthesis is supplied by Gregory of Nyssa who sees man's carnal condition as a deviation from his original status as the image of God. While the body is the source of man's sensible affections which are usually perverse, these tendencies can be combated by ascesis whose motivation is supplied by a striving for *apatheia* and, thence, the reformation of God's image in man, leading to contemplative union with God in ecstatic love.

St Athanasius, on the other hand, conceives of man as endowed from creation with a spark of divine grace (*charis*) which he lost in the fall. He has thus tumbled down into the baseness of created being (*phusis*) which is good in itself, but corruptible. He is now weighed down with concupiscence in a multiplicity of worldly cares, bad habits, and a false sense of liberty which keep him from ascending to God by ascesis and contemplation (*Contr. Gen.* 2-4; *De Incarn.* 3-6).[8]

4. CONCUPISCENCE ACCORDING TO THE LATIN FATHERS

With Tertullian, Hilary of Poitiers, Ambrose and Jerome, the western fathers generally follow a dualistic anthropology and locate the course of concupiscence in man's affections. While considering internal bodily movements as natural, they speak of tendencies towards uncontrolled indulgence as the result of weakness induced by original sin. Man's freedom consists in his ability, with grace, to direct these natural movements away from the suggestions of the devil and through self-denial to the exercise of virtue.

Pelagius denied that original sin was the source of concupiscence and considered the root of sinfulness in bad habits inherited by the human race from imitation of Adam's disobedience. Augustine in reaction to the consequence of this over optimistic view of human nature, insisted upon original sin as the root of a damaged, vicious quality in man's nature that has so weakened his moral liberty that he is incapable without grace of keeping God's commandments as he should (*Contr. Jul.* 5; *de Nupt. et concup.* 2, 23). Even after regeneration through baptism, man is still the subject of concupiscence in both body and soul. Combining Pauline doctrine with his own sinful experience, Augustine is pessimistic in his views of man's inordinate appetites. In particular, he relates concupiscence to sensual and sexual desire (*Contr. Jul.* 3, 51; *de Nupt. et concup.* 1, 2) and thus influences later patristic and early medieval thought (Faustus of Riez, Maximus the Confessor, Gregory the Great) to consider sexual concupiscence as the cause of original sin.[9]

5. CONCUPISCENCE ACCORDING TO MODERN MORALISTS

Modern Catholic theologians since Trent have followed two divergent courses in explaining the effects of concupiscence. All agree on three elements that enter into consideration: the inordinate movements of the appetites (sensible and rational); the necessity of grace; and the liberty of choice between good and evil. Some, with Pascal and the older French Oratorians stress the evil effects of original sin which manifest themselves in concupiscence as a rebellion of man's human desires. They see the remedy in a rigouristic self-denial and a repudiation of all worldly satisfactions.

Others, with St Francis de Sales, insist more on man's ability with grace to channel the urges of concupiscence towards good works which emanate from man's love of God and of his neighbour. Each school recognises the danger in pushing its contentions to an extreme. Each likewise insists on ascetical practices, prayer, and self-denial as necessary to overcome the results of concupiscence.[10]

Contemporary theologians see in concupiscence a natural phenomenon that existed in man when endowed with integrity and original grace, but which now, because of the damage brought about by original sin, inclines man more towards evil. Others ask whether the essence of concupiscence does not consist in a fundamental opposition between wounded nature as such and man's restored, supernatural destiny. Regeneration in grace removed the guilt of sin, but it has not fully repaired human nature's innate orientation towards the supernatural. This is the source of an existentialist anxiety—the *lacrymae rerum*—that can only be overcome by a return to a consciousness of the *hokmah* or wisdom of God within man.

The effort of the early Church to adapt its ethical concepts to the diverse religious and secular knowledge *vis-à-vis* the human experience of *epithumia* should serve us as an example of moral pluralism in our endeavour to update Christian moral teaching today.

Notes

1. See F. Murphy 'The Background to a History of Patristic Moral Thought' *Studia Moralia* 1 (1963) 54-61.
2. H. Jaeger 'The Patristic Concept of Wisdom' *Studia Patristica* 4 (Berlin 1961) 93-98.
3. W. Jaeger *Early Christianity and Greek Paideia* (Camb. Mass. 1975) pp. 3-12; *Id. Paideia* 3 (Oxford 1944) pp. 149f., 224-227.
4. See C. Baumgartner 'Concupiscence' *Dict. Sp.* 2 (1955) 1334-1373.
5. J. Daniélou 'Demon' *Dict. Sp.* 3 (1955) 162-163; 168-174.
6. P. Wilpert 'Begierde' *Relig. Ant. Christ.* 2 (1954) 62-78.
7. G. Wingren *Man and the Incarnation* (Eng. trsl. R. McKenzie, London 1959) 50-63.
8. M. Spanneut *Le Stoicisme des Pères de l'Église* (Paris 1957) 170-178; F. Murphy 'The Moral Virtues in Patristic Thought' *Seminarium* 3 (1969) 412-415.
9. A. Solignac 'La Condition de l'homme pécheur d'après saint Augustin' *Nouv. Rev. Theol.* 78 (1956) 359-387.
10. K. Rahner 'The Theological Concept of Concupiscence' *Theological Investigation* I (London 1961); J. Metz 'Begierde' *Lex. Th. Kirche* (2nd ed. 1958) 108-112.

Wilhelm Ernst

The 'Classical' and 'Modern' Foundations of Ethics in the Middle Ages

IN THE contemporary discussion of theologically legitimate forms of ethics, one often meets a division of ethics into 'classical' and 'modern' ethics. For many people this classification also implies an evaluation. According to their view classical moral theology as it was developed by St Thomas Aquinas and handed on and taught in the Church for centuries is the standard for every form of ethics, so that a modern form of ethics can only be regarded as legitimate to the extent that it can be brought into agreement with classical moral theology or at least reconciled with it. The basis for this fairly widespread view, one that is also put into effect in practice, is the conviction that Christian ethics can only have validity as a uniform kind of ethics and that therefore in comparison with classical moral theology every other conceivable form of ethics is to be regarded as an unjustifiable deviation.

The aim of the following remarks is to show that, within the framework of the development of fundamental moral theology considered from the point of view of the history of theology, this kind of uniformity has neither existed nor is demanded but that as early as the high and late middle ages different forms were developed of the rational justification of ethics and could thus claim a legitimate place within the doctrine of the Church.

1. VIA ANTIQUA—VIA MODERNA

In the second half of the previous century intensive effort went into investigating the attempt to establish and maintain a modern approach in the fourteenth and fifteenth centuries in distinction from, and to some extent in sharp contrast to, classical doctrine.

Most older research, and particularly those authors who saw themselves more closely linked to the methods and doctrinal approach of the ancients transmitted by St Thomas Aquinas, saw in the intellectual and doctrinal approach of the moderns, especially that stimulated by Duns Scotus and William of Ockham, the beginning of the dissolution of scholasticism and the medieval concept of order, the precursor of humanism and the Reformation, the forerunner of the rationalism of a Descartes or a

9

Leibniz as well as of the empiricism based on sense-data that was to develop later in England and France.[1] Some authors accused these moderns of every conceivable error: exaggerated suprarationalism in theology, scepticism in ontology, empiricism and mechanical atomism in natural philosophy, materialism in psychology, subjectivism and individualism in the study of man, and in ethics formalism, voluntarism, moral positivism and semi-Pelagianism.[2]

More recent research into the doctrinal approach of the moderns, on the other hand, reaches conclusions that allow us to talk of a certain revolution in their evaluation. According to this research the doctrine of the moderns is to be considered in a far more differentiated manner than was the case in previous research.[3] Their intellectual approach cannot be squeezed into a uniform pattern, nor can they simply be described with the label 'nominalism' with the negative overtones that term has carried from the fifteenth century until today. At the time of its origin the moderns' intellectual approach was a matter of the scientific method that enabled teachers in the course of giving instruction to pass on the material they were teaching in a new and modern way. In the fourteenth century the moderns were called 'terminists' because they rejected the realism based on universals of the ancients. Later they were described as 'real conceptualists' because they attacked Averroism and radical Aristotelianism. The name 'nominalists' was only generally attached to them in the fifteenth century, and then by their opponents, the 'realists', who accused them of excessive speculation in philosophy and theology as well as of rejecting clear statements of St Thomas.[4] William of Ockham explicitly rejected the term 'nominalism' for his teaching, and the later moderns preferred to call themselves Ockhamists after Ockham or Gabrielists after Gabriel Biel, hardly ever nominalists. In contrast to many present-day interpreters, in the fifteenth century people were quite clear that the term 'nominalists', even though it was intended as a polemical description, did not include the accusation of a theory that would see universals as mere sounds (*flatus vocis*), since this—what is described as nominalism in the strict sense—had already been worsted in intellectual debate by around 1350. The fact that what was involved in the 'moderate nominalism' advocated by the moderns of the fifteenth century was an intellectual approach reconcilable with the teaching of the Church is shown by the fact that at several universities, for example Tübingen, Basle, Heidelberg and Salamanca, both approaches were represented and given equal honour in the chair of the *reales* and the chair of the *nominales*.[5]

2. BASIC ATTITUDES AND PRINCIPLES OF THE MODERNS

The real distinction between the ancients and the moderns emerges from demonstrating the basic attitudes and principles of the moderns.

The basic attitude is neither a negative scepticism aiming at a radical separation of philosophy and theology, nor an exaggerated hankering after novelty that attempts to throw overboard the enduringly valid contents of valid doctrines of the Church and in their place to introduce new and daring theories. Rather it is the effort, in a world that in fact is undergoing change in all spheres, to press forward to an understanding of the relationship between God and man in which both the limits and the possibilities of human reason must be demonstrated. The aim was precisely by this means to allow the radical difference of God and man to emerge more clearly as well as the validity of the truths of revelation that cannot be comprehended within any human pattern or ordering. The change in the understanding of the relationship of God and man, of absolute and created being, that was already beginning to emerge in the theology of the thirteenth century is the reason why among the moderns of the fourteenth and fifteenth centuries the central point in their reflections, with special emphasis on God's immediacy, was held by stress on the principle of God's absolute power and on the idea of contingency as well as by an examination of the traditional classification of things. The experience of a world in which what exists is contingent and in which human perception can only rarely achieve permanently valid statements about God and the world led important theologians of this time to call man himself and his perceptual knowledge into question and on the basis of revelation to ask what man was before God and how in his pilgrim state he could find the path to salvation.[6] This basic attitude is closely connected with the basic principles that were consistently championed by most of the moderns as positive guiding principles as well as negative correcting principles: the principle of contradiction, the principle of omnipotence, the principle of causality, the principle of parsimony (Ockham's razor), and the principle of contingence. What they mean is that for God all things that do not entail any logical contradiction are possible. Everything that God can bring about with the help of secondary causes he can also bring about and maintain immediately and without their help. God can bring about and maintain every reality, whether substance or accident, without another reality. No plurality or multiplicity is to be accepted without necessity. Every genuine reality distinct from God is to its innermost core contingent.[7]

It should be fairly obvious that a particular kind of fundamental moral theology arises from these principles, even if it does not arise exclusively from them.

3. DIFFERENT MODELS IN THE CONCEPTION OF ETHICS

In contrast to the present, medieval theology knew neither a separation of dogmatic and moral theology, nor in its considerations of ethical questions did it start from the question of moral obligation and its ultimate rational justification. Questions of moral theology were discussed entirely on the basis of the Christian belief in God that was taken for granted in the Christian world of that time and the moral order that had its basis in God. But the concept of God itself provides the foundations for different models of theology and of moral theology. Admittedly none of the theologians of that time doubted the fundamental real identity of God's essence and his attributes, but with the help of distinguishing between virtual, formal and conceptual qualities St Thomas Aquinas, John Duns Scotus, William of Ockham and their followers reached a different accentuation of God's understanding (wisdom) and will (omnipotence). This difference of emphasis then had its effects on God's relationship to his creation and on the rational foundation of the moral order.

4. THE INTELLECTUAL MODEL

Let us begin by considering St Thomas Aquinas's conception of ethics. This is usually labelled intellectualist. In interpreting his teaching we must of course be aware that there are nearly as many different interpretations as there are interpreters. But at least there should be agreement on the fact that St Thomas Aquinas incorporated his conception of moral theology totally within his dogmatic system and understood man's path to God in a pattern of exodus and return. Man, created by God and redeemed in Christ, is ordered to the good as his object and end. The supreme good is God, and hence he is also man's supreme and ultimate end. The man who lives virtuously finds in the bliss of being with God his ultimate fulfilment and perfection. In this sense St Thomas's ethics is an ethics of the virtues.

This pattern of exodus and return is linked by St Thomas with his doctrine of law, the interpretation of which is a matter of remarkably strong dispute today. For the idea of the natural moral law that is in question here the decisive element according to St Thomas is God's *ratio*. The emphasis on God's *ratio* is the decisive element in St Thomas's total attribution to the divine *ratio* of the eternal law which was developed by the Stoics and reshaped by Augustine and which provides the rational foundation for the moral law of nature. The eternal law is the law of divine reason as the guiding and ordering principle and point of reference for everything that is created. Corresponding to this the natural moral law as a sharing in the eternal law is the law of reason of man created in the image of God. Because of his rational nature man takes an active part in the *ratio* of the divine wisdom. Man is not merely in the position of recognising this law as the law of what he ought to do, but this law itself also obliges him to be actively concerned for himself and his fellow-men in a rational manner. Human reason is thereby man's real law-making capacity: it is the origin of moral obligation. This means that no obligation of any kind can be imposed upon man that is not dictated by reason, since moral obligation is based exclusively on man's moral insight and not on any commandment imposed on him from outside.[8] In this sense we can, without coming too close to Kant's idea of a pure practical reason, talk about a genuine moral autonomy of the reason, though of course in this the ultimate basis for moral obligation is for St Thomas to be understood as derived from God's *ratio*, since his theological starting-point is the order of creation.

The reason for natural reason dictating moral obligations is to be found on the one hand in man's relationship to the good and on the other hand in the constitution of his being as someone created in the image of God. The good is the object and end of human existence. Hence it is justifiable and rational to trace human existence to its end. But since man's ultimate end is perfection in the bliss of heaven, St Thomas is able to say that man's proper moral obligation consists of moving towards happiness, that is the contemplation of God, in a virtuous life. In this way St Thomas thought he had established the link between *beatitudo* and *obligatio*. In discovering what on this path is morally binding one needs according to St Thomas to take notice of what are termed the natural tendencies to self-preservation, to reproduction, to the formation of community and to the search for the truth. But according to St Thomas, in contrast to many later Thomist interpreters, these tendencies do not yet have any normative character, that is they do not in themselves provide any moral norms, but are morally relevant in the sense that they are the material, the context for the establishment of norms by the practical reason. Again in distinction to many later interpreters, particularly neo-scholastic ones, St Thomas includes in the unalterable primary natural law only the primary principles of behaviour, while the secondary rules of behaviour derived from them he attributes to the sphere of the changeable secondary natural law.[9]

To sum up, the decisive basic elements of the Thomist conception of ethics can be stated as follows: the doctrine of the good, of the virtues, and of man's perfection in blessedness, which Thomas understands as supreme knowledge; then the emphasis on God's *ratio* in the *lex aeterna*; and finally the rational basis, justification and structure of the moral order. The primacy of reason is emphasised in all the decisive points of this conception of morality.

The conception of ethics developed on the foundations demonstrated by St Thomas was considered up to the present as the proper 'classical' moral theology, although it should not be overlooked that within this conception there is a multiplicity of modifications that extend to the present day through the various treatments to be found especially in Gabriel Vázquez, Francisco de Suárez and the neo-scholastics of the nineteenth and twentieth centuries.

5. THE VOLUNTARIST MODEL

In contrast to this 'classical' conception of moral theology, medieval and late medieval theology, starting especially with Duns Scotus and William of Ockham and his followers up to his most important pupil Gabriel Biel, developed a conception of moral theology whose advocates were impelled by the same concerns as St Thomas Aquinas but with the emphasis not on the primacy of intellectual perception and knowledge but on the primacy of the will and on a freedom that depended on the radically undetermined nature of the will.[10] Since what is thus termed voluntarist ethics is often liable to misinterpretation, some explanations are needed of this concept to show the origins of the term.

To begin with, voluntarism in the sense of Scotus and Ockham is not to be understood as introducing a gulf between essence and will in God. There is no justification for the view that for Scotists and Ockhamists God's essence is absolute will and not, as with St Thomas Aquinas, thought. According to Scotus and Ockham God's will is really identical with his essence, even if formally or nominally distinguished from it.

Further, voluntarism in the case of Scotus and Ockham should not be understood as if God's external activity were something arbitrary. That would mean that both the natural and the moral order would depend on a purely arbitrary will or whim of God, and this in the sense that God would have created an arbitrary moral order in keeping with his own pleasure. When Scotus and Ockham say that good as well as evil are entirely dependent on the will of God, this is to be understood against the background of the principles that have already been mentioned and that in their case are key concepts of their theological methods. God's external activity does not take place of necessity and according to eternal ideas deposited in his reason, but is instead free. The one limitation on his power, but at the same time its condition, is the principle of contradiction. There is no contradiction in God freely choosing in an eternal decision the order that he wishes to establish in time. This kind of free establishment does not contradict his justice, which is indeed identical with his essence, nor is the natural and moral order established by God an irrational order, for God cannot do anything irrational. God's reason has brought it about that natures are what they are. God's will, however, has freely chosen from the infinity of rational possibilities those that ought to have been created. 'If God had created other natures, there would also have been good and evil, but nevertheless it would not have been the same. If God's wisdom had established other natural laws or if God's justice had established other moral laws which would have been in agreement with the substance created by him or with those that he could have created in their place, there would have been another natural or moral order which would have been no less just and wise than that which we know, and nevertheless different from it.'[11] According to Duns Scotus there can be no irrational whim in what God accomplishes. Not the essence but in fact the choice of every rational order depends on his will.

Without admittedly advocating a psychological order in God like Scotus, the Ockhamists take a similar line when they emphasise that there is a rationally founded natural law but that the choice of moral order is a free act of God. The voluntarism that is to be understood in this manner is theologically legitimate from the point of view of its understanding of God's relationship to man, even if it is the object of many theological controversies.[12]

Finally, voluntarism is not to be understood as an arbitrary handling of the established order, since God has tied himself to the natural and moral order he has established. Hence according to Duns Scotus God can only do what is not irreconcilable with the order he has established. God could never command anyone to hate him. On this point Ockham does not want to see anything affecting God's absolute sovereignty. Theoretically he regards the possibility of hating God as conceivable (*de potentia Dei absoluta*), but in practice excludes such a possibility as ethically indefensible.[13] The later Ockhamists do not follow their master in holding this view but adopt the Scotist theory instead.

In comparison with St Thomas's conception of ethics one can label this model of moral theology voluntarism and moral positivism. But Scotus and Ockham would both oppose such a classification and would point to the fact that they too teach that the good has its foundation in God. But against St Thomas they would assert that the good cannot simply be defined from nature, understood as a reflection of the divine essence. Hence for them ethics becomes 'not the doctrine of the behaviour that, thanks to an eternally valid order of being, "naturally" corresponds to man created according to an eternal idea, but the doctrine of what God in his freedom, through his actual will, has commanded man to do'.[14] In this sense one can say, particularly of the Ockhamists, that in their moral theory the obligatory character of what is commanded by God is stressed much more strongly than in the case of St Thomas Aquinas.

One cannot, however, describe this conception of ethics as simply a morality of obligation. On the basis of their theological starting-point the advocates of the voluntarist tendency are particularly interested in the question of what laws are ordered as necessary and sufficient conditions for our salvation. For them the answer is provided by the determination of the relationships between the natural moral law and the revealed decalogue. Like St Thomas Aquinas they too recognise first practical principles that are known by themselves. Their truth is necessary, with the result that God himself cannot bring it about that what they command as good can become evil and *vice versa*. They are always and universally valid and constitute the natural law. From this arises the question whether all the commandments of the decalogue necessary belong to the natural law. St Thomas Aquinas answered 'yes' to this question; but he declared that the commandments of the second table were to be understood not in the strict but in the broader sense, since God could dispense from them. Such a conclusion is inconceivable for Scotus and Ockham. As is shown by the history of salvation, God has in fact dispensed from the commandments of the second table.[15] But since he cannot dispense from the natural law, because if he were to do so he would contradict himself, the commandments of the second table do not belong at all to the natural law. Behind this assertion stands the view that a commandment only forms part of the natural law if the good it prescribes is linked by a necessary relationship to the good of the ultimate end. But in this sense only the first two commandments of the decalogue form part of the natural law, since the natural law that one must do what is good necessarily entails that one must love the highest good, God. All the other commandments of the decalogue are not necessarily entailed by this law and therefore do not in the strict sense form part of the natural law. Admittedly, the commandments of the second table do to a high degree correspond to the natural law, but they are not necessary deductions from the first principles. Hence they are not absolutely necessary but hypothetical, in other words as conditions ordained by God for the achievement of salvation.[16]

Here it becomes clear once again that the voluntarist theory of morality has its basis in a definite understanding of the relationship between God and the world. On the basis of this understanding moral theology is developed as the theory of the order established by God for behaviour that leads to salvation. Man himself has complete freedom to determine that he will pursue this goal set him by God. He cannot be obliged or constrained to pursue this goal by anything, neither by his intellect nor by any other point of reference.[17] From this point of view one can in fact talk of voluntarism. But from this one may not conclude that there could be a voluntarism with regard to the moral determination of behaviour. From this point of view there is only an intellectualism, since the moral rightness of an action consists of its agreement with the correct judgment of reason. In this both schools are in agreement.

6. CONSEQUENCES FOR SUBSEQUENT AGES

Contemporary discussion of the two models of ethics that have meanwhile been expanded and modified has already been mentioned at the start of this paper. All that remains to be said in conclusion is that in the Reformation there was a total break between the models of ethics presented here and the ethics of Martin Luther. On the basis of his completely different intellectual approach Martin Luther, who became particularly acquainted with the Ockhamist school in Erfurt, rejected both tendencies. In the intellectualist school he saw nothing other than an Aristotelianism dressed up in theological clothes with an overemphasis on the metaphysical order of being and obligation. In the case of the voluntarist school he rejected particularly the freedom of the will *coram Deo*. Nevertheless it should not be ignored that he includes strong echoes of the concept of God and of the understanding of man such as were advocated in the voluntarist school.

The extent to which the emphasis on the individual, the character of obligation and the supremacy of the will has influenced subsequent moral philosophy is something that can in detail only be demonstrated with difficulty. But what does not seem to be excluded is that ethics conceived in terms of command and the ethics of casuistry are closely connected with the development of which the clearly marked manifestation in the late middle ages was the voluntarist conception of ethics. In the development of the Church's teaching at the Council of Trent, as in neo-scholasticism, the intellectualist school prevailed. Even in the different interpretations to be found today it forms the basic model to a greater extent than the voluntarist school.

Translated by Robert Nowell

Notes

1. See H. Hermelink *Die theologische Fakultät Tübingen vor der Reformation 1477-1534* (Tübingen 1906) pp. 104, 133.

2. A good example of this view is to be found in F. X. Linsenmann 'Gabriel Biel, der letzte Scholastiker, und der Nominalismus' in *Theologische Quartalschrift* 47 (1865) 460. See also C. Feckes 'Die religionsphilosophischen Bestrebungen des spätmittelalterlichen Nominalismus' in *Romische Quartalschrift für christliche Altertumskunde und für Kirchengeschichte* 35 (1927) 204.

3. See among others E. Hochstetter *Studien zur Metaphysik und Erkenntnislehre Wilhelms von Ockham* (Berlin/Leipzig 1927); P. Vignaux s.v. 'Nominalisme' *Dictionnaire de théologie catholique* XI, cols. 717-784; H. A. Oberman *The Harvest of Medieval Theology: Gabriel Biel and Late Medieval Nominalism* (Cambridge, Mass. 1963); W. Ernst *Gott und Mensch am Vorabend der Reformation. Eine Untersuchung zur Moralphilosophie und -theologie bei Gabriel Biel* (Leipzig 1972) and the literature cited there.

4. A useful survey is provided by E. Kleineidam *Universitas Studii Erffordensis,* part I (Leipzig 1964).

5. See W. Ernst in the work cited in note 3, at p. 119.

6. See W. Ernst, *ibid.* pp. 79ff.

7. See W. Ernst, *ibid.* pp. 77, 81.

8. See the interpretation by H. Reiner 'Wesen und Grund der sittlichen Verbindlichkeit (obligatio) bei Thomas von Aquin' in *Sein und Ethos. Untersuchungen zur Grundlegung der Ethik* (Mainz ed. P. Engelhardt 1963) 236-266.

9. See A. Hertz 'Das Naturrecht' in *Handbuch der christlichen Ethik* ed. A. Hertz, W. Korff, T. Rendtorff, and H. Ringeling (Freiburg-im-Breisgau/Basle/Vienna 1978), I, p. 327.

10 On Duns Scotus see E. Gilson *Jean Duns Scot: Introduction à ses positions fondamentales* (Paris 1952).

11. E. Gilson, in the work cited in the previous notes; quoted from German translation *Johannes Duns Scotus. Einführung in die Grundgedanken seiner Lehre* (Düsseldorf 1959) p. 633.

12. See W. Ernst, the work cited in note 3, pp. 87ff., 197.

13. For a discussion of this problem see W. Ernst, the work cited in note 3, pp. 125, 199, 201.

14. L. Grane 'Biels Lehre von der Allmacht Gottes' in *Zeitschrift für Theologie und Kirche* 539 (1958) 70.

15. Always cited at this point are the well-known examples from the Old Testament. The dispensation consists of God replacing the existing commandment by another that corresponds better to the situation.

16. The hypothetical character of the commandments does not mean that they do not entail an absolute obligation. Under the conditions established by God they are absolutely binding.

17. The concept of freedom that is decisive for the voluntarist school cannot be explained in more detail here. According to St Thomas the will is determined by the intellect. In this the voluntarists see a form of determinism. For them it is inconceivable that the will as the active and more distinguished faculty should be determined by the intellect as the passive faculty. According to Duns Scotus the freedom of the will is to be put at such a high level that in the face of the clearly observed final end and by means of *caritas* it can be raised up, but not compelled, to will it.

Clodovis Boff

The Social Teaching of the Church and the Theology of Liberation: Opposing Social Practices?

1. THE TERMS OF THE QUESTION: MORALITY AND ETHICS

IN GENERAL terms, the question is to establish the difference—if there is one—between a morality inspired by the Social Teaching of the Church (STC) and one inspired by the Theology of Liberation (TL). Both form less than completely homogeneous theoretical constructs. Even their usual titles pose some problems, and they should probably always be referred to in quotes. But for present purposes, we can take the usual titles as expressions of broad indications of thought and action in the social field.

First, however, we need to distinguish between morality and ethics. Morality is acting rightly in a given situation, while ethics is right thinking about how to act. So the distinction is between theory and practice. But how are the two related?

Morality (practice) is based on 'laws', either unwritten (conscience) or written (ethical codes). This is of the essence of moral activity, which, in effect, means following a series of ideas, values, commandments, etc. But this is only one part of the truth about morality, since both morality (practice) and ethics (theory) depend on social conditions and reflect social interests.

If this is so, it is not enough simply to say that a particular ethical system (such as might be found in the STC or the TL) will inspire particular codes of social behaviour. We also need to see how such codes of behaviour influence the ethical system or are expressed in it. There is a circular process of interaction here. Furthermore, moral teaching reflects practice rather than the other way round. This can be seen from the fact that differences in morality (practices) and ethics (theories) among Christians generally correspond to differences in their social standing and understanding.

2. THE PRACTICAL INFLUENCE OF THE STC IN ECCLESIAL PRACTICES

What social behaviour is inspired by the ethics contained in the STC, what *ethos* does it produce?

17

What is plain to see is that in Latin America (to which I shall confine this study) the Social Teaching (or Doctrine) of the Church is little known and therefore also little followed. It could not possibly be called the 'soul' of pastoral practice in the Latin American Churches. But the STC does inspire interest in the following circles:

(a) the Christian Democrat parties. These were in fact set up as a direct and specific expression of this teaching;

(b) certain reformist currents in Catholic Action, such as, to take an example from Brazil, the Association of Catholic Employers;

(c) base movements as well, but in a different sense. In fact the many base movements, particularly the Basic Ecclesial Communities (BECs), take their basic points of reference straight from the gospel, not from the STC. As for the TL, this gives an articulate form to this basic reference and so gives it greater coherence and weight. There is, however, a dialectical relationship between the BECs and the TL. Broadly speaking, the BECs are to the TL what Christian Democracy is to the STC: its best expression in practice.

So what is the relationship between these basic Christian movements and the STC? They do not reject it, and it serves three purposes:

(a) It is used to *sensitise* the public at large to social questions. It does this through sermons, lectures, classrooms, catechesis, courses, etc. The STC has, as a matter of fact, a particular stamp of authority: it is the voice of the 'supreme pastor of the Church' and represents the will of the bishops, the 'shepherds of the People of God'. The STC has always shown its power to win people and groups over to the cause of social justice and, at least, to gain sympathy for the Church's stance on the side of the poor and the oppressed. In effect, the STC poses the problem of social justice fairly and squarely, thereby superseding the narrow concepts of charity as almsgiving and faith as an option affecting one's private life.

(b) The STC is further used to provide a doctrinal *justification* for certain stances taken by the Church when these are attacked in public. It provides an ecclesial basis for certain lines followed by Christians in pastoral and social practice. Its effect when used in this way is proven, particularly when those—including governments—who attack the social practices of the Church, lack the necessary intellectual equipment to face up to the Church on equal terms.

(c) The STC is just and useful in *confirming* and strengthening the actions taken by BECs and similar groups. Such groups are frequently encouraged by references to the STC by popes and bishops, and particularly by those of the pope on his recent visit to Latin America.

So the role of the STC in BECs and similar organisations is threefold: sensitising, justifying and confirming. This threefold function brings out certain strands in the teaching more strongly than others, as we shall see later. But further than this it cannot go: it is incapable of standing up to reality to an adequate extent, let alone of transforming it. So here we have to ask: why is the STC incapable of being a doctrine that can take root in the movement of transforming history? Why does it not lift Christian spirits in the fight against injustice? Why does it lack the mystic appeal of, say, Marxism, or sometimes nationalism? Why can Christians see themselves in it but not feel affected by it? Even in the case of Christian Democracy, its most obvious inspiration is in fact liberalism (as seen in its endless defence of the 'sacred cow' of private property) rather than the STC. And as for those Christians today most committed to social change, it is significant that they do not look to the STC for the basic motives for their inspiration and struggle.

This is in fact what happens when one approaches the STC: one finds that it agrees with practically everything. But once its texts have been studied, practically nothing stays in the mind. This is true of public opinion when a social encyclical comes out; opinions are roused, positions taken. But it does not take long for the document to be consigned to oblivion, with the exception of one or two paragraphs, and these continue to be its only links with the mind. So, for example, *Pacem in Terris* has left that passage opening up the possibility of co-operation between Christians and non-Christians in the social field, and linked with this, the famous distinction between 'doctrine', which is unchanging, and 'historical movement', which can change. *Populorum Progressio* still means the statement, which has today become a commonplace, that 'the poor are becoming ever poorer and the rich becoming ever richer' (no. 57), the condemnation of naked capitalism (no. 25), and the possible legitimation of 'revolutionary uprising' (no. 31). *Octogesima Adveniens* left above all in Latin America an openness to socialism (no. 31), the excellence of political work as an example of loving service (no. 46) and the appeal to lay people to act creatively on their own initiative in the social field (no. 48). And so one could go on with them all.

The fact is that the encyclicals and social documents gradually became identified with a certain number of inspirational nuclei. The same historical process of doctrinal selection meant that Medellín came to be BECs and the 'option for the poor'. So instead of appearing as a completely assembled machine (system) the STC rather resembles a box of spare parts, from which just these teachings, these historically significant abbreviations, can be picked out. The rest vanishes from consciousness and from history, though it clings on in books and lectures.

3. THE SOCIAL ETHIC OF THE THEOLOGY OF LIBERATION

The distinctive features of the social ethic set out and put forward by the TL to groups of committed Christians can be summarised as follows:

(*a*) *in theory*: the adoption of principles of social analysis. Reading the Signs of the Times has become an ethical-political requirement for the BECs and similar groups. Society can be changed only on the basis of knowledge of this society. In this sense, Marxist analysis is used as a theoretical instrument, with the greatest freedom and responsibility in theory and practice;

(*b*) *in history*: an alternative society to capitalism. It is clear to the TL and the BECs that this social system cannot provide a way to overcome the exploitation and oppression. So social change is understood as a break with the present system in force. In this sense, what is put forward is a revolutionary morality (changing the system), not a reformist one (change within the system). Socialism is the more or less explicit aim;

(*c*) *in practice*: class organisation of the exploited. They are seen as the protagonists of social change. They should be joined by each and every member of other classes to the extent that these are disposed to take on the cause of the exploited, to serve them and not to make use of them.

4. THE SOCIAL ETHIC OF THE SOCIAL TEACHING OF THE CHURCH

In order to tackle this thorny question, one has to decide how the STC should be viewed. It is possible to see it from two totally different viewpoints, which lead to two equally different hermeneutics: one seeing the STC as an open system and the other as a closed system.

(a) The STC as an open system

Understood in this way, the STC is not found completely wanting, but it is inadequate, incomplete from the point of view of social practice. This means that:

(i) *in theory*: the STC does not, and does not claim to, give a scientific explanation of social reality. It only offers general principles, criteria and orientations of an ethical nature. So, when it affirms that the State is the mediator of the common good, it is expressing an ideal (ought to be) and not a given situation (actually is). So this is not an analytical, but an ethical judgment. Scientific and technical analysis of social problems is properly said to be the task of lay people (see *Puebla* 85, 793, 826);

(ii) *in history*: the STC does not claim to propose social models (see *Oct. Adv.* 24, 25, 42), but just a Christian view of humanity and society (see *Puebla* 472, 475, 525, 539). By presenting a Utopian goal of a just and fraternal society, it opens the ethical field (and only this) to specific historical embodiments. On the other hand, Christians are encouraged to work with others in devising other, alternative models of society (see *Oct. Adv.* 48; *Puebla* 553, 1211);

(iii) *in practice*: the STC calls all social agents to act, each in its own field. And when it defends the right of classes to organise in support of their rights, particularly the working classes, and when, more recently, it takes up the refrain of the 'option for the poor', one can see what direction its thoughts are moving in.

Looked at in this way, there is no contradiction between the STC and the TL. On the contrary, the former stands in relation to the latter as the theological field in which the latter can logically be situated. There would be a dialectic between them of the determinant (STC) and determined (TL). The TL would be a 'historical determination' of the more general doctrinal guidelines and practical criteria of the STC. So the TL would in no way suppress the STC but would advance beyond it dialectically. There would be a dialectic of continuity between the two, always determined, nonetheless, by the primary reference of both to the gospel. But even so, the STC would form a first approach or mediation between the gospel and a given social situation—a mediation open to subsequent theological determinations.

Furthermore, the further down the hierarchy of *magisterium* one goes, the greater the accord found between the STC and the TL. So, for example, there is virtually only a formal distinction between the social documents produced by the Brazilian National Bishops' Conference and the Brazilian works of the TL. This is the case with the document, 'The Church and Land Problems' issued by the Bishops' Conference in 1980, both the form and content of which 'beat' with the basic ideas of the TL and the BECs in general. Often, there is no discernible difference between the pronouncement of a single bishop and an approach of the TL; this is the case in a recent declaration by the ex-president of CELAM, Cardinal Aloisius Lorscheider: 'The socio-economic system adopted in our countries is a sinful, anti-evangelical system, in need of deep change, which implies a structural change of the system. . . . A "Yes" on the part of the Church to the socio-politico-economic system at present in force in our lands will never be possible, since the Church cannot, in conscience, regard as evangelical what is structurally contrary to God's plan' (*Folha de São Paulo*, 4.12.80, p. 6).

So, we can see that the TL has no difficulty in linking itself with an open concept of the STC. Rather, it can be enriched by it, just as in turn it can enrich it.

(b) The STC regarded as a closed system

Understood as a system that is complete in itself, the STC appears to be a sort of 'Catholic *summa* of economic and social questions', as *Mater et Magistra* described *Rerum Novarum* (no. 16). It would thus be a theoretically self-sufficient system. So:

(i) *in theory*: whether consciously or not, the STC includes a social theory. Its *forte*, however, is ethical, based primarily on natural law. Here its ethics implies a more elaborate social analysis, which tends towards theoretical totalitarianism. This is the conclusion one must draw from this sort of statement: The Church 'does not need to have recourse to ideological systems in order to love, defend and collaborate in the liberation of the human being' (John Paul II, in his inaugural address to Puebla, quoted in *Puebla* 552); 'Catholic workers do not need to seek social guidelines from other ideological sources. The Word of Jesus Christ, recorded in the gospels and interpreted by the social teaching of the popes and the Council, in matters concerning employers as well as the workers themselves, contains all that is necessary to man for his happiness on earth and to guarantee him his dignity' (Paul VI, to German workers, 30.4.71). This tendency can be called 'theologism': it rejects any outside mediation on principle. Nevertheless, when it is submitted to practical application, the STC is obliged to incorporate vehicles of social understanding. If their implications are critical and radical, the STC rejects them as alien; if they are bureaucratic and conservative, the STC in applying them produces effects contrary to its own principles: in theory it is anti-capitalist, but in practice it collaborates with this system. And if the ethical principles of the STC are applied without any outside framework, then the disaster is complete: 'Application of the STC leads firms to bankruptcy', as the Catholic Employers' Federation told Mgr Ivo Lorscheiter, the present president of the Brazilian Bishops' Conference.

So the STC is incapable of moulding history in accordance with its own principles. As a self-sufficient totality it is contradictory: its (objective) effect is on a collision course with its (objective) intention. It wants to remain purist—'a spotless virgin, but barren', to quote Bacon. In his famous *The Social Teaching of the Church and Christian Groups*, E. Troeltsch showed that pure evangelism led to historical irrelevance and social insignificance. *Dato non concesso* that there can be purity in these matters, except possibly in intention. . . .

(ii) *in history*: the STC, as an overall viewpoint, sets out the ideal of a 'juster and more Christian society', a 'fraternal society', a 'civilisation based on love'. Here Utopia is taking over from any specific proposal for a historical plan. This is why the STC tends to regard other forms of social plan, such as socialism, as competitors. And to reach this 'juster society', the STC does not think in terms of a break with existing patterns, but of gradual reforms, which are nevertheless qualified as 'deep' and 'urgent', in correcting abuses and changing mentalities;

(iii) *in practice*: the STC, still seen as an exhaustive view of society, appeals to all classes without distinction, including the poor. . . . Its philosophical (ethical-analytical) view of the State as guardian of the common good, naturally assumes that the protagonists of change will be those who hold power—at any given moment, naturally. Seen functionally in this light, its social ethic is reduced to de-ontologising, that is, to a professional ethic. Try to be a good capitalist, or a good worker, not to wipe out the corresponding class differences. . . .

So, understood in this way, the STC can find itself in opposition to the TL, and vice-versa, just as the social (political-moral) practices of the proponents of each—'liberal Christians' and 'committed Christians'—can oppose each other.

5. AN OPEN RELATIONSHIP IS REQUIRED

While only a short time ago the dominant view of the STC was that of a closed, complete system, there are now increasing signs of a growing change towards an open view of the same system. I have already referred to these. To sum up:

(*a*) the existing pronouncements of the STC are now being used on the level of commitment to change, particularly its historically relevant doctrinal points. These are taken to define the *minimum level of consciousness* required of Christians today. The STC is adopting a more historical viewpoint and therefore a more critical one—as can be seen from its *changeable* and perfectible character (*Oct. Adv.* 42; *Puebla* 472);

(*b*) the STC is coming to be understood as a continuing process and one that is more and more being expressed in the social pronouncements of bishops' conferences, or of individual bishops. This shows its broad and *dynamic* character (*Puebla* 473);

(*c*) finally, the STC is coming to be understood as a first specific mediation, though still a very general (and therefore incomplete) one, between the gospel and our times. In this, it shows its *openness* to later determinations, including the TL.

Only such an understanding, with its corresponding hermeneutic, can allow the STC to be related correctly to the TL. This is precisely the line being taken by the theological endeavours in Latin America today. These theoretical endeavours are simply the reflection of the practical tendency of a Church which, as a whole—hierarchy and laity, *magisterium* and theologians—is putting itself increasingly *in partibus pauperum*.

Translated by Paul Burns

Eric Fuchs

Sociological and Theological Differences in 'Catholic' and 'Protestant' Morality as Seen in their Confrontation in a Denominationally Mixed Country (Switzerland)

SWITZERLAND IS obviously an excellent field of observation for the study of Christian pluralism. Switzerland is a veritable microcosm of western society, in which there is confrontation between four languages, two religions (as people say in our country when referring to the two Christian traditions, Catholic and Protestant, a fact which is not without interest in measuring how far the denominational difference is interpreted in terms of a difference in life-style) and two cultural areas, the Germanic and the Latin. As such, it has had to learn, in order to survive, the harsh realities of pluralism. For many years the differences which distinguish the Protestant and Catholic cantons from each other have been observed. Thus, whenever the Swiss go to the polls (a frequent event in our country!) the denominational division has political consequences. These are indirect in the case of elections, where the unified strength of the Christian Democrat party, which is supported by most Catholics, contrasts with the diversity of the non-denominational parties (Radical, Liberal or Socialist) which are in power in the Protestant areas. The repercussions are far more direct when the voters are consulted on issues which imply, more or less directly, a choice of the form which society is to take: on every occasion, the Catholic cantons are distinguishable by their resistance to change and their attachment to traditional values.

Even if it is necessary to modify more and more carefully these 'Weberian' reflections on Protestant attachment to progress and Catholic conservatism, since so many other factors must be taken into account today in a society which is as secularised and liberal as western European society, it is none the less true that pluralism, especially where questions of morality are concerned, is a fact of life in a country like Switzerland, and as such it is a fertile source of useful information. It allows us to undertake observations at a variety of levels. First of all, at the level of an overall assessment which is concerned with determining the way in which this pluralism is revealed in the personal or collective life-style of the members of the two traditions. Then, at the level of a more precise analysis which seeks to discern the exact composition of ethical pluralism: theological and non-theological elements, those things which witness to positive values and those which stem rather from psycho-sociological motivation. Finally, the level of value judgment, which must inevitably be carefully balanced, for if pluralism is potentially capable of making a rich contribution to Christian ethics it also, on the other hand, poses some difficult questions which are impossible to avoid.

1. AN OVERALL ASSESSMENT

We are concerned here with the understanding of the principal features of the dual Christian ethic when pluralism is the cause of a permanent critical confrontation, which naturally results in a strengthening of the characteristic features of each denomination.

What characterises the *Catholic* moral attitude is surely the fact that it appears to be determined from the outside, by an authoritative teaching to which the believer must submit himself. The 'moral law' from which he seeks guidance is presented as a comprehensive formal structure, which is not contingent and which must be obeyed. Governing, at least in certain privileged areas such as sexuality, the details of the believer's existence, the moral law enunciated by the Church does not, in principle, call for any personal interpretation or re-examination which would modify its application. This point of view obviously puts a premium on obedience rather than liberty, and on those values which encourage the incorporation of the faithful within a framework of teaching rather than those which involve the risk of individual questioning. This corresponds at the collective level to a more disciplined political attitude amongst Catholics and their enrolment in an institutionally visible expression of the Church's desire to group the faithful together in organisations bearing the Catholic label (party, trade union, school, cultural or sports club, etc.). Lastly, the Catholic areas are characterised by the effective collaboration which links the political and religious authorities and, despite the secularisation by which it is threatened, maintains a structure of Christendom which is certainly more resistant than Protestantism to the assaults of modernism.

The bourgeois form of modernism was more favourable to Protestantism which, moreover, had produced it. It is possible that the new form of modernism, which is more responsive to major social developments (in economics, the information industry and ideology) may be more favourable to the Catholic ethic, since it allows it to demonstrate more clearly its powers of resistance.[1] Where issues concerning social morality are involved, Catholicism seems much better equipped to resist the pressures of conformity which are to be found in contemporary society.

Another element which should be noted at this level is the apparently paradoxical relationship which can be seen between the tightly disciplined framework offered by Catholic morality and its optimism concerning its followers' capacity for obedience. It is through obedience that man fulfils his ultimate vocation. Never contradicted, this anthropological viewpoint remains basic, for it is from this that morality receives its full importance, its nobility even, since it is the way whereby man participates in his 'salvation'.

If we now turn to *Protestant* morality, considered, as we have previously stated, from an overall viewpoint, to reveal its principal features, we find immediately that morality is presented as the inner acceptance, ceaselessly renewed, of the values proposed by the law of God in Scripture. It is a battle which must be won over and over again, against a background of conflicts and uncertainties. It supposes and demands personal responsibility. The latter is the final court of appeal which no human or ecclesiastical law can be allowed to dominate. The Protestant does not expect the Church to dictate his conduct, but to remind him of the gospel, that is to say of the pardon which is free, undeserved and unattainable by our human works. This is because he knows that he is threatened, like the divided man whom Paul describes in Romans 7:13ff, with succumbing to the endless torments of scrupulousness, which paralyses action and reduces morality to a collection of good intentions which reality constantly contradicts or derides. One tendency of Protestant morality does undoubtedly lead to this rather sickly introspection which makes morality the paradoxical reason for never committing oneself to action because it is seen to be so full of ambiguities. But what seems more significant to the observer is the desire for personal rigorousness which is characteristic of the Protestant. 'There are some things which are just not done', not simply for reasons of conscience but also, and perhaps especially because we are, each of us at his own particular level, responsible for maintaining and securing a social order which is both possible and peaceable.

In Protestantism, morality depends less on a saving obedience than on a formative educational process. This is why it cannot be expressed in a formal law, and still less by one which has a casuistical form. It can never lose its character of parenesis, moral exhortation, which seeks, with the help of examples, to arouse the free responsibility of the subject; it is nourished by the twofold conviction that salvation does not depend on the exercise of this responsibility, since it is, on the contrary, the reason for it, but that responsibility bears witness to the seriousness of a man's awareness of that salvation. 'Seriousness' is, no doubt, the word which characterises most aptly the Protestant ethic. One recognises here, but in reverse, the paradox we discerned earlier in Catholic morality: Protestantism has no confidence in man, or in his obedience; sin is never overcome, in the sense of being left behind in the past: it remains present as a form of man's limitation, fragility and idolatry: *semper peccator et justus*. And yet, Protestantism calls its followers to a lucid exercise of their responsibility, as if everything depended on them. This is because its objective is not to change society, and even less to change man, but to bear witness to the ultimate value of that which fosters the moral act, that is, the gospel or at least the certainty of the irreducible status of the conscience. The rigour, which is rather 'uptight', of the Protestant sets itself no other goal than the agreement of the conscience with the ground of its being. This produces an individualism which fears, in anticipation, the group (the Church) which might come between its conscience and its God, but it also produces the courage which takes risks. Whereas Catholic morality seeks to be the expression of a Church in order to create a Church, Protestant morality seeks to produce people who are capable of resisting—even the Church!—when the truth held by conscience is at stake.

2. FROM SOCIOLOGICAL ASSESSMENT TO THEOLOGICAL ANALYSIS

Our examination of moral pluralism has so far been conducted from the outside, as it reveals itself particularly through denominational contrasts which are still very apparent in a country like Switzerland. But such a description has left to one side the question of the validity of these two contrasting forms of Christian life. In order to be in a position to appreciate the theological value of this pluralism it is first necessary to seek to understand which emphasis each of these two moral traditions wishes to convey, and whether these different tendencies are irreconcilable or complementary.

We must confine ourselves to the essentials. In so far as *Catholic* morality is concerned, I believe that its fundamental theological emphasis can be shown by describing it as a permanent struggle on behalf of the objectivity and the universality of the moral law. This fact is well known. The Revelation, which the Church has the responsibility of communicating, is the revelation of the possibility of the fulfilment of the potential of natural man. Grace is not so much a judgment as a bringing to fruition. 'Thus there is in man no possibility of two separate moralities, one purely human and the other supernatural: the first is subsumed by the second. Acts which are naturally moral are brought into the service of the supernatural life and are given value by it.'[2] What is being emphasised here is both the objectivity of morality, based on the recognition of the importance of the theology of Creation, and the magisterial function of the Church, without which natural morality would remain in ignorance of how it is called upon to fulfil itself.[3]

Why is it necessary to defend the objectivity of the moral law? In order to safeguard from any interference or distortion those 'fundamental human values' which are revealed to faith by studying the example of Jesus Christ.[4] Man does not need to be invented so much as to be recognised, on the basis of the creative intention of God; this recognition defines the perspective of the eschatological fulfilment. It may certainly be pointed out—as Protestant authors have not failed to do!—that this kind of basic position inevitably produces a conservative attitude in practice, but one may also underline the fact that this kind of defence of objectivity is alone able to guarantee the fruitfulness of the critical dialogue between ethics and the human sciences. It involves, aided by the human sciences but without subscribing to all their ideological presuppositions, a quest for something which might become a theological anthropology, defining structures of existence which must be respected if distortions are to be avoided.

The *magisterium* has the task of constantly reminding men of this objectivity, recognised in the final analysis by faith, but seen to correspond to 'basic concepts of human reason' (Ratzinger). To wager that at some point the revelation of the truth of man in Jesus Christ coincides with the best results of scientific research, and therefore to invite theologians and scientists to collaborate in the construction of a humanising normative morality, would thus seem to be the positive aim of the magisterial function. There still remains, however, in the eyes of the Protestant theologian, the question of the power which that *magisterium* claims for itself in the name of a so-called objective knowledge which does not derive from faith but does not depend on science either, since only the Church can state what it contains. It is at this point, no doubt, that non-theological factors have a very real influence. It is clear that the confrontation of moralities in the midst of what is in fact a pluralist society reveals the ambiguousness of the status of the *magisterium* of the Church in the sphere of morality. It seems sometimes that this *magisterium* is more involved in the defence of the Catholic institutional structure than with the faithful and hazardous preaching of the gospel.[5]

Let us turn now to Protestantism. *Protestant* morality, in the different forms which it has adopted, defines goodness in terms of right relationships. With God first of all—the theme, which is central to the Reformed tradition, or justification; then with others—the primacy of love, that is, of concern for people in real terms; lastly, with oneself—the theme, so strongly developed by Calvin, of sanctification. An ethic which is not so much dependent on an objective good as animated from within by the faith of the subject, covered by the recognition of God's goodwill towards us over against the recognition of the profane condition of the world, which must be made holy to the glory of God.

Protestant morality may be characterised as personalist and critical. Personalist, because it implies a personal relationship of faith with God and His Word, to which Scripture bears witness through the inward illumination of the Holy Spirit. There is no true morality without a decisive personal commitment concerning the ultimate meaning of existence. Critical, because—the original suspicion with regard to any theology of works!—morality can only attest by analogy the reality of the coming Kingdom. Comparing the two moralities, Catholic and Protestant, André Dumas writes: 'In the first case, nature coincides in substance with Revelation. Nature contains within itself, in spite of sin, in spite of the passions, in spite of the distance between the primitive order and present reality, a sub-stratum (which is rational and vital) which is the ground of the natural law, as the Church helps it to emerge (. . .). In the second case, nature coincides eschatologically with Revelation. Nature is journeying towards that time when the particularity of the Church will disappear in favour of the universality of the city of God.'[6]

Thus there may be discerned, from the Protestant viewpoint, a dual basis for moral action: the intimate conviction of the subject, assured of his right relationship with God, and the desire to intercalate in the profane nature of the world some signs of the Kingdom which is coming, both as fulfilment and as judgment. This emphasis on the moral subject, called in some way to invent morality in the light of the permanent critical perspective of eschatology, is obviously intended to protect the liberty of love from the temptation of legalism. And also to combat any attempt to consider as sacred any form of historical or social contingence, in the name of the sole Lordship of God—*soli Deo gloria*. Such a position may, it is true, lead to relativism or conformity, when the subject no longer recognises the source of his conviction or when the critical attitude degenerates into an impatient refusal of reality; this is what Catholic criticism has often emphasised when attacking Protestant morality! But it can also inspire the recognition of the irreducible status of the moral conscience.

This exaltation of the subject is often accompanied, it is true, by a loss of the sense of the world and its reality; when the gospel no longer seems to concern anything other than the inner spirituality of man, no longer setting him in the context of a world which is recognised as the locus of a summons and of a transforming activity. This weakness of Protestant morality, especially in its modern form, is due, no doubt, to the specifically theological difficulty which it finds in grafting a theology of the Word onto a theology of the body, an eschatology onto a sacramental system of symbols. The regrettable outcome of this one-sidedness is always to reduce the Word to the Scriptures and to ensure through the written word the objective authority which it has failed to find elsewhere. Fundamentalism, with its moralising consequences, is the Protestant disease. . . .

3. THE VALUES OF MORAL PLURALISM IN ECUMENICAL EXPERIENCE

How are these two traditions, of which we have just described the theological background, lived out today in the local situation of the churches of a country like Switzerland, in the new ecumenical climate which has been in existence there for the past twenty years or so? Before answering that question, let us note that in those places where this ecumenical experience is lacking, pluralism is still lived in terms of opposition. The two traditions mutually drive each other back towards their extremes, as if the best way of affirming one's Protestantism or Catholicity consisted in a systematic refusal of the values emphasised by the Catholics, or the Protestants, respectively! This fact is worth noting: pluralism only proves fruitful if it is lived in a climate of mutual welcome and recognition. Otherwise it results in a hardening of attitudes, in a caricature of morality imposed as a condition of membership of the group (for instance, morality as found in the Protestant sects, or as seen by Mgr Lefebvre). What is specifically Christian is lost: this may be seen in Switzerland where, in such a case, Catholicism tends to align itself with political conservatism and Protestantism with economic liberalism. Pluralism which takes the form of juxtaposition functions as the most powerful means of support for the *status quo*, without calling it in question.

In contrast, lived out in an ecumenical climate, this same pluralism becomes a source of enrichment. Why? Because each of the two traditions emphasises one basic element of the Christian scheme of things which, as it happens, the other has neglected. It is clear that the quest for a universal objectivity which would base morality on anthropological facts which cannot be interfered with or distorted has belonged within the Christian tradition from the beginning. If the churches of the Reformation have neglected this issue, it was because they were concerned to stress the responsibility of the subject. But we very much need to learn that the subject is not a pure potentiality, but the locus of expression of a psychological and social structuration. Similarly, Catholicism had eventually forgotten that only faith can reveal the reality of the real, in the name of which it becomes possible to invent, on the spot, new ways of obedience instead of tracing from afar plans which are abstract because of a concern for universality. Let us put this in another way: it is important that the Protestant tradition should learn from Catholicism the gravity of the ontological question as a condition of the Church's ability to withstand demoralisation, and it is necessary that the Catholic tradition understands from Protestantism the seriousness of the issue of the irreducible status of the conscience.

This mutual questioning is complemented by an internal debate, in which each tradition is compelled to reconsider its own nature, in the light of what the other tradition has revealed to it.[7] This self-questioning inspired by the reality of pluralism has resulted in the appearance of a new division which, this time, is not denominational but runs through each of the denominations. On one side are found Christians (who are in the minority in the Swiss churches) who, in ethics, stress the eschatological criticism of institutions (political, social, economic and ecclesiastical), on the other Christians (who are undeniably in the majority in our churches) who expect their churches to strengthen these same institutions by affording them a religious justification. From certain points of view this new division, which creates very considerable tensions, is experienced more harshly than the previous one, to which we had grown accustomed with time. It is thus that moral pluralism, recognised as a positive element thanks to the new climate of relationships created by ecumenism, is becoming transformed and is asking questions of all the churches on their social and ethical function in a society of material and technical abundance which is, however, unstable and uncertain of its identity.

This new pluralism, whose consequences and demands, in a country like Switzerland, are far from having been fully appreciated, liberates the ethical debate from its denominational localisation; it cuts across the boundaries of all the churches in the *oikouménè*. In our opinion, it has inaugurated a new stage in the history of Christian morality. Between the values of integration and the values of protest the debate is renewed on a universal scale. It would be regrettable if attempts were made to reunify, too rapidly or by coercion, this new pluralism which, it may be hoped, will be a fertile influence on the life and the thought of all the churches.

Translated by L. H. Ginn

Notes

1. One might perhaps interpret according to these categories the recent development of the Catholic Church. Whereas Vatican II represented an attempt to align Catholicism with liberal democratic modernism, the present pope seems less concerned with 'modernising' Catholicism than with making it capable of resisting the new technocratic modernism, if necessary even by means of doctrinal simplifications.

2. J. M. Aubert 'Evangile et droit naturel selon l'enseignement de l'Eglise catholique' in *Pratique du droit et conscience chrétienne* (Paris 1962) p. 39.

3. 'The knowledge of natural law is possible through the powers of reason alone, but this often involves so many difficulties and imperfections. On the other hand, through the light of Revelation, the regulations of this law are seen in a new way, which shows thereby the close and vital relationship which exists between the natural order and the order which springs from the gospel', J. M. Aubert in the article cited in the previous note, at p. 60.

4. We are both making use of the terminology of J. Ratzinger, in J. Ratzinger and Ph. Delhaye *Principes d'éthique chrétienne* (Paris-Namur 1979) p. 129.

5. One example, which seems to us to be significant, of this confusion between moral authority and institutional power is the way in which Paul VI promulgated the encyclical *Humanae vitae*; see on this point P. de Locht *Les Couples et l'Eglise* (Chronique d'un témoin) (Paris 1979).

6. 'La Théologie de Karl Barth et le droit naturel' in *Pratique du droit et conscience chrétienne* (Paris 1962) pp. 94-95.

7. This phenomenon may be observed on reading the proceedings of a conference on ethics organised by the Universities of French-speaking Switzerland: *Loi et Evangile* (Héritages confessionels et interpellations contemporaines) directed by S. Pinckaers and L. Rumpf (Geneva 1981). The Protestant theologians ask questions about the legacy of the Reformed tradition and P. Gisel, proclaiming the necessity of an ontology, argues against the interpretation of J.-L. Leuba as too Lutheran. As for the Catholic moralists, they are seeking ways of moving beyond legalism. As S. Pinckaers says: 'the Catholics, tired of hearing about the law, are seeking today a remedy, as if this were something new, in the primacy which should be accorded to faith, charity, the Holy Spirit and His charismata, the gospel, liberty and the individual conscience, and they use these at times as battering-rams to attack the walls of the Law. The Protestants, for their part, warned by their own experience, are rather suspicious of all these terms which evoke certain abuses from which they have suffered, and they prefer, without in any way abandoning these things, to seek a certain measure of solidity in the Law and its commands'. (At p. 253.)

Julia Ching

Ethical Encounter:
Chinese and Christian

THE SUBJECT of ethical encounter between Chinese wisdom and Christian ethics may be discussed on two levels: the historical one, dealing with all that has already taken place, and the theological one, dealing with similarities and differences between the two traditions, as well as possibilities of future interaction. In this article, it is my aim to begin with the historical encounter, move from it to the theological or normative, and then return to the historical—or rather, look at the *recently* historical, with a view to formulating possibilities regarding future encounter. Such a plan suggests already my functional definitions of Chinese wisdom, not only in terms of the traditional, Confucian-inspired moral philosophy, but also keeping in view the 'new moral wisdom' in the making—I refer here to the evolving moral values of modern and contemporary China, especially since the Communist takeover in 1949. I shall keep similarly in mind a 'dipolar' perspective of Christian ethics, as the traditional Catholic moral philosophy as well as an evolving, more 'pluralist', post-Vatican II morality. To do so, I shall begin with a contrast between the *images* projected in the West by Chinese wisdom in the past, especially in the seventeenth and eighteenth centuries, and the *realities* observed by missionaries, then and afterwards. After this, I shall proceed to an analysis of Chinese ethical wisdom—both the traditional wisdom of Confucian-dominated China, and the more modern wisdom of Communist China, attributed till recently to Mao Tse-tung. I shall discuss the question of a common ground with Christianity while looking also towards the future.

1. FROM THE PAST: IMAGES AND REALITY

Traditional China called herself, and was known by her nearer neighbours, as the land of virtue (*li-yi zhi bang*). Her high ethical standards were especially proclaimed in the Confucian classics—notably the Five Classics (Books of Change, Poetry, Rites, Documents, and the Spring-Autumn Annals) and the Four Books (Analects, Mencius, Great Learning, Doctrine of the Mean). While she was geographically distant from Christian Europe, the European mind was sufficiently well disposed towards this far-off land. Some believed it to be the Christian kingdom of Prester John, the perennial figure, representing European projections of themselves in the non-European world—a land of pious and virtuous co-religionists. This myth actually echoed a fact—the historical presence of Nestorian Christians in China, in the seventh and eighth centuries and lasting long afterwards, although always as a small minority. This fact only came to light in the early seventeenth century, when Jesuit missionaries were working in China—after the brief Franciscan effort of the thirteenth century. This new upsurge of missionary activities during the seventeenth and eighteenth centuries in turn provoked keen philosophical interest in the newly discovered Orient, called the land of Cathay. Intelligent Europeans had become better informed, through an outpouring of edifying and curious letters from China, as well as early simplified translations into Latin of selections from the Chinese classics. Such European luminaries as Leibniz, Wolff and Voltaire all made some serious efforts to understand China, using as their sources the missionary accounts and translations, and taking part in controversial debates regarding Chinese philosophy and religion. Of these persons, Christian Wolff made the most of Chinese ethical wisdom. He had to leave Halle (1721) after delivering there his controversial lecture, *De Sinarum Philosophia Practica*, in which he highly praised this non-Christian—and, to him, atheistic—philosophical tradition based on human reason and the example of nature. He openly acknowledged there the harmony of Confucian teachings with his own moral philosophy regarding the efficacy of human reason in meeting the problems of daily life. And he emphasised that there was no essential conflict between such a moral teaching and Christian doctrines. His beliefs were also affirmed by Voltaire, who extolled Confucian morality for its preference for moderation, seen as the quality of the gentleman, in opposition to the excessive asceticism identified with 'medieval' Christianity. The English deists belonged to this school of thought, and Matthew Tindale interpreted Confucius' moral code as an ally to Christianity. Wolff—as also did Quesnay—made much too of Confucian political ideals, as can be seen in his later lecture (1750) on the 'Real Happiness of a People living under a Philosopher King'.

The modern scholar may find these eulogies excessive and uncritical, compared to the more tempered judgments of Montesquieu and others. The differences of opinion voiced by missionaries themselves on the subject of Chinese virtue and wisdom, point to possible exaggerations—whether of praise or blame—for the purpose of 'persuasion', especially for the sake of 'winning' public intellectual opinion over to one or the other side during the Chinese Rites controversy over whether Chinese converts might be permitted to continue to participate in traditional Chinese rites, including the ancestral rites. History, however, tends to repeat itself. In the recent decades of our twentieth century, before the People's Republic of China 'normalised' its relations with the outside world, we witnessed the 'new missionaries'—frequently ex-missionaries—once more divided in their opinion of China and her new Maoist wisdom, tending frequently to excessive praise or blame, in the absence of more reliable information. The Cultural Revolution (roughly, 1966 to 1976) was especially a case in point. Some praised it for its populist, egalitarian thrust, even for bringing about a secular kingdom of God on earth and creating a 'new man' dedicated to the service of the Chinese people in particular, but also to humankind at large. Communist China became, for many enthusiasts, a Utopian alternative to western capitalism and Soviet bureaucratism. The disillusionment came about only lately, with the trial of the 'Gang of Four', who were 'at the helm' in those days, and the disclosure of political and moral chaos wrought by them. Another dream is being dissipated—a western projection of what she wanted China to be.

If these have been the 'images' of China to the western world, what are the realities? Is she a nation of sages or of scoundrels? The answer, of course, is at once far and near. Common sense reminds us that there can be no nation of either sages or scoundrels, human nature being what it usually is. And common sense happens to be the foundation of much of what is called Chinese ethical wisdom, both of the past and the present.

2. CHINESE ETHICAL WISDOM

To speak in general terms of a tradition over two millennia long, one may characterise Chinese wisdom by its organicity—the interrelatedness and interpenetration of its many parts within the whole, an interrelation so complete and thorough that the detachment of any one part from the whole could lead to distortion. In such a tradition, the various levels of reflection, whether metaphysical, epistemological and ethical, are all integrated, to be found one in the other, and frequently expressed in a language which is noted for its multivalence.

However, a discussion of Chinese *ethics* is possible and fruitful, so long as the difficulties involved are not overlooked. The Chinese language possesses the equivalent terms for ethics, *lun-li xue*—the study of the principles of moral relationships, and the more informal *dao-de xue*—the study of the Way (Tao) or fundamental moral principle, and its manifest virtues (Te). Both are associated particularly with the school of Confucius, for long China's reputedly greatest sage. It proposes a form of altruism which gives consideration to special relationships of blood and duty. This is best represented by the doctrine of *ren* (Jen), 'human-heartedness', a universal virtue, that which makes a person truly human. This word *ren*, itself a homophone of the word 'human', is written with the radical 'human' and another word signifying the number 'two'. It points to man's social nature, his relatedness to other men. The gentleman, the true man, practises a 'graded' love which assures a special attention to his parents and children and other family members, as well as to his sovereign and friends—to each according to his due. His relationship to *all* others is governed as well by a golden rule, in a formula which offers a strong echo to the Christian equivalent: 'What you do not wish others to do unto you, do not do unto them.' (*Analects* 12:2). Mencius, Confucius' most famous follower, has offered an empirical ground for morality, that of moral feeling based on human nature and its spontaneous, even instinctive, choice of the good in moments of crisis which call for altruism. The best example he gives is that of someone seeing a child fall into a well, and *instinctively* rushing over to attempt some rescue, before arguments of self-interest could arise. Upon this foundation of moral feeling, Mencius has built his doctrine of human perfectibility, of the possibility of all attaining the highest ideals of sagehood and virtue. Mencius' moral optimism is especially reflected in the moral philosophy of Wang Yang-ming (1472-1529), who came nearly two millennia later, and taught that human nature and the human mind and heart possesses within itself the ability to know the good as well as to do it. He is referring not to certain and innate knowledge of the good but rather a power of moral discernment supported by that of moral fulfilment.

Such optimism did not go unchallenged: Mencius by Hsün-tzu (c. 300 BC), and Wang Yang-ming by many of his own contemporaries and later thinkers. But the general consensus of Confucian ethical wisdom has been on the side of moral optimism and human perfectibility—notwithstanding what one's belief regarding the *original* inclination of human nature may be—whether towards good or evil. But if *political* corollaries are to be inferred, my observation is that those of Mencius' persuasion are actually more vocal in urging for a benevolent or humane 'philosopher-king' (or 'despot') ready to heed the advice of his philosopher-ministers. Those of Hsün-tzu's persuasion—that human nature itself is evil, although capable of transformation through education and culture—have been more supportive of authority in general, whether of the State or the home, as well as of the sanctions accompanying it.

This simple representation of Chinese ethics, done in bold strokes, overlooks many controversial and finer points. Some of the questions it might arouse could be answered later, when comparisons with Christian ethics are made. In *continuity* with the past, contemporary China, having opted for a Marxist form of government and orthodoxy, has made efforts in a quest for its own 'materialist ancestry', found allegedly in certain aspects of the Taoist or Confucian legacy. Chinese Marxists have tended to side more with Hsün-tzu than with Mencius, articulating the human propensity for evil as well as the possibility of perfecting human nature by education or 're-education'. Chinese Marxists have praised the teaching of 'universal love', proclaimed by Mo Ti (c. 400 BC), a radical altruist, on account of its egalitarian overtones, while they have criticised Mo's explicit religious beliefs and voiced occasional approval for Confucius' relative silence in this regard. Of course, Chinese Marxism—sometimes called Maoism—is more than just another Chinese school of thought. It is also Marxism: explicitly atheistic, promoting class struggle in the name of social equality. In its regimented society, the rallying cry of 'Serve the People' directed principally to the building of a socialist society in China itself, offers resonances to other lands as well.

3. ANY COMMON GROUND?

As recorded above, traditional Chinese philosophy focused its attention on the problem of good and evil in human nature, and arguments proffered by both sides revealed a fundamental agreement concerning human perfectibility. But there was no systematic inquiry into a related issue—that of freedom and moral responsibility, upon which the whole ethical enterprise rests. This brings to light an important difference between Chinese and western philosophies. Chinese thinkers have largely been content to keep silence over such problems as God's existence, human freedom and spiritual immortality—problems that many westerners admit as insoluble but continue to investigate. However, silence need not be construed always as a denial of the importance of the concerned issues. Chinese thinkers never denied or argued over the evidence of common sense. Their articulation of ethical principles is itself a clear proof of their acceptance of moral freedom and responsibility, much as the moral teaching of the New Testament presupposes the same, without offering any formal analysis of these presuppositions.

The *doctrine* of human perfectibility presents a point of convergence as well as of divergence for Chinese wisdom and the Christian tradition. The explicit, Christian horizon of sin and grace, of justification by faith—and works—is not part of the Chinese heritage, although this does not necessarily mean the Chinese did not have a *sense* of sin, and a felt need of some form of justification. In this respect, and according to our recent experience, Chinese converts have generally found an excessive focus on man's sinfulness on the part of the missionary Church, which contrasts with the optimistic tradition of Confucius and Mencius. Since the Second Vatican Council, a noticeable change has occurred in the theological concerns, as a more positive view of human nature and human fulfilment replaces the former, pessimistic attitudes. Nevertheless, even the secular western society tends to be preoccupied with the problem of human wickedness in its literature as well as in a society ridden with violence. In this respect, it is interesting to note that Marxist China has derived from a *western* ideology its own persuasion of human propensity to evil, which it finds confirmed in the tradition of Hsün-tzu. Chinese Marxist optimism in human transformation is also western-derived, but probably strengthened by the traditional Chinese belief in perfectibility.

Is there a Chinese equivalent to what Christians call Natural Law? I refer here to a sense of justice, said to be placed in human hearts by the Creator. From what has been said above, the answer is Yes, whether the Chinese call it so or not. The difference regards the Creator as Lawgiver. The problem of God's existence, as well as those regarding his creative and law-giving activities, have not been as important in the Chinese tradition, and both theists and atheists, as well as pantheists, may be found among Chinese philosophers of the Confucian tradition. The main thrust of the Chinese tradition has, all the same, been directed to the discovery of the Absolute in human relationships, and the virtue of *ren* acquired an absolute dimension in a process of evolution, as love became identified with life, including cosmic life.

As suggested earlier, the philosophy of Mo Ti, which once rivalled that of Confucius, appears to offer more parallel to Christian beliefs and teachings concerning God's existence as well as the radical love of one's neighbours. Christian missionaries recognised this similarity, and assisted in promoting a revival of interest in Mohism. Marxist scholars have likewise acknowledged Mohist egalitarianism as an important philosophical legacy, to be 'isolated' from its theism. If, however, Mo Ti never acquired the popularity of Confucius and Mencius, it could be on account of his extreme demands on human nature. Christianity, on the other hand, preaches radical altruism but expects it only of a few. In a sense, Chinese Marxism—Maoism—repeated the Mohist demands on human nature, only to find that it too had to compromise with reality and common sense or run the risk of becoming mere hypocrisy.

So far, the discussion has remained on the level of theory, and theory offers much yet for exploration. But while the doctrine of perfectibility implies a basic human equality, the doctrine of proper human relationships, as enunciated for example in the school of Confucius, emphasises social hierarchy, and the dominance of the ruler over the subject, the father over the son, the husband over the wife. The Marxist revolution came also as an agent of social change, expressing disapproval for such traditional attitudes. But it nearly substituted *one* patriarch for all the fathers and husbands, in exalting the cult of the Leader. This phase being now over, a secularised West discovers in China a newly secularised East, bereft of many of its beliefs, seeking once more to reconstruct an ethical superstructure in the wake of the destructive Cultural Revolution. Quite obviously, the new China has not yet found a viable, new form of ethical wisdom and is still engaged in its quest.

4. WHAT FUTURE?

What future might one speak of, for an ethical encounter between Marxist China and the Christian West? Paradoxically, the answer lies partly in the fact that China *is* post-Confucian, and in some respects even post-Marxist, just as the West might be described as *post*-Christian. As already mentioned, China is still searching for a viable, new form of ethical wisdom; so is the West. In spite of the different experiences of East and West in the remote as well as recent past, each finds itself in an ethico-religious situation which is very similar. Each faces an uncertain future. In each case, many have found *tradition*—whether that be Christian or Confucian—wanting. The Chinese attempt to *radically* 'uproot' its own Confucian past has been disastrous, and voices are now being raised in favour of a 'critical' evaluation and selective inheritance of the ethical tradition of the past. The western experience has also been of conflict: between a minority of traditionalist Christians more eager to preserve the past than to adapt to the present or prepare for the future, and a larger number of those who recognise the critical nature of a society in change, and the need of re-examining values and life-styles previously taken for granted. The *fact* of Communism in eastern Europe, and the *challenge* of Marxist ideology in Latin America, serve also to prepare the West—western Europe and northern America—to understand better today's China.

And so: has China anything to teach the West, or is she rather in the same situation as the West?

I think that the recent upheavals in China—including the moral vacuum, or the 'ethical' upheaval related to it—shows that the Chinese experience has its universal relevance. The lessons may be described as both positive and negative. *Negatively*, China has shown the world that human nature does not change overnight, that the most powerful political leader cannot make 'a new man', that ethical values are not created by *fiat*. *Positively*—if this be the right adverb—China has also demonstrated a certain solidarity with the rest of the world—joining with the rest of us in this quest for values in a time of uncertainty and change. In the remote as well as more recent past, China has tended to favour doctrinal orthodoxies—whether Confucianism or Marxism—and their monolithic value systems. She has tried them and found them somewhat wanting, because the needs of the time have changed so much, and continue to change rapidly. She has sought to replace one value system with another, and found the results disastrous. She is realising that a viable ethical superstructure must allow for both continuity and change, that it must permit some kind of pluralism: the kind that makes up, in political terms, a 'United Front'.

Is not western Christianity confronting a similar situation of finding a proper balance between continuity and change, of acknowledging the reality of pluralism, of finding value in a pluralism of ethics? Traditional ethical values, like Christian faith itself, were, to a large extent, *inherited* more than they were chosen. But mankind today, whether in the East or in the West, is confronted with the need of making serious choices from moment to moment, both collectively as well as individually. Can the world's resources support an uncontrolled population growth? China's certainly cannot, and the political leadership is urgently promoting responsible controls—in a country which had previously considered the bearing of children, especially male heirs, as the topmost duty of filial piety towards the ancestors. On the other hand, the dicta of the deceased Chairman Mao Tse-tung, previously (more recently), considered as sacred, indeed, infallible and wonder-working, have been relativised. In its wake, moral decisions have become once more an individual responsibility rather than blind obedience to authority. Has this not also been the recent experience of western Christians, who had previously expected and received from a hierarchical Church—as especially in the case of Roman Catholicism—prescriptions and proscriptions regarding moral behaviour for both individual and social life?

Ethical encounter between Chinese wisdom and Christian morals is all the more interesting today, because of this common quest for pluralism, a quest based on the lessons of history as well as the needs of the present day.

Georgette Odi Assamoi

The Family in African Tradition and Christian Moral Teaching: Contact and Conflict

WHEN THE missionaries landed south of the Sahara, in the steps of the explorers, they saw no outward signs of civilisation, but only forest and savanna. The proud empires of earlier centuries had collapsed, leaving behind no pyramids or splendid monuments. So the newcomers concluded that historically and culturally this was virgin territory.

But the land was inhabited, and the missionaries in their burning zeal to bring the Good News to these new-found sons of Adam, following the command of Christ himself to go and teach all nations, faced boldly up to every danger. So began the great venture into the unknown from which the African churches were to spring.

However, since it had been decided that there was no indigenous civilisation, it is impossible to speak even of contact between African tradition and Christian ethics at the beginning. Any signs of indigenous custom were viewed with suspicion and severely punished. Gradually, however, the resistance encountered led to a developing awareness that here was something different, until today it is being asked whether Africa may not after all have its own contribution to make to world civilisation. The Church itself is asking the same question.

The historical summary just given provides the background to this article and the questions implicit in its title. What tradition of the family and family life did the Christian missionaries encounter in their attempt to evangelise the Africans? Have this tradition and the Christian ethic had any influence on each other? Have there been any efforts to adapt them one to the other? To put it differently, what are the greatest difficulties an African experiences when he tries to live out his Christian faith without breaking from the traditional pattern of family life?

We shall treat the subject in two stages, first presenting the African tradition of family life with its constants, characteristics and values, and second, discussing some of the problems encountered by Africans who try to live, amid their family, in accordance with their belief in the person of Jesus Christ.

1. THE FAMILY IN AFRICAN TRADITION

In order to preserve some unity in the material we shall be dealing with, and because our knowledge of other parts of the continent is limited, we shall restrict our discussion to Black Africa. Even so, is it not in fact presumptuous to speak of just one African tradition of the family? How dare anyone treat as a homogeneous entity such a multiplicity of ethnic groups and tribes, when even in a small state like the Ivory Coast we have sixty or so ethnic groups whose traditions vary considerably? However, beneath the diversity of language, ethnic group and tribe and the great variety of tradition, there are undoubtedly certain elements common to all Africans.

The reader must not expect to find here a detailed monograph about a particular tribe, which we are not qualified to undertake; in any case the work has already been done, by eminent sociologists, ethnologists and anthropologists. We do not claim either to be giving a complete picture or an exhaustive description of everything the expression 'the family in African tradition' may be taken to cover. But on the basis of our own knowledge, acquired by study on the one hand and by experience on the other, we shall be attempting to present what we trust will be an accurate and representative idea of that tradition.

(a) Characteristics and structure of the family

When an African speaks about the family he never means the nuclear father-mother-children unit. For him, the family includes all the descendants of the same ancestor. Depending on the system followed in the region, this ancestor may be a woman or a man. In the matrilinear system, the line starts from a woman and passes through her daughters to their daughters, and so on. In the patrilinear system, the line starts with a man and passes through the sons and their male descendants. Both systems are found in Black Africa, but whichever one they live under, Africans like any inhabitant of Planet Earth know that it takes a man and a woman to produce a baby.

So the family is made up of generation upon generation of parents, grandparents, uncles, aunts, male and female cousins, brothers, sisters, nephews and nieces; a vast group whose members all meet together only on occasions like a death, since they do not necessarily all live in the same village, and even less in the same family compound. Although the nuclear family is starting to become more important and independent as our society changes, the term 'African family' always refers in this article to the extended family described above, the very size of which is the first feature that distinguishes it from types of family found elsewhere.

(i) Kinship

Membership of a family is based on descent from a member of the family. However, depending on whether the local system is matrilinear or patrilinear, the mother or the father is more important. In a matrilinear system, a woman's children have higher standing than her brother's children. But her brother's children have comparable standing in their mother's family, in which they are a woman's children. So lower status on one side of the family is compensated for by higher status on the other. In consequence, individuals will tend to frequent the side where they rank higher.

(ii) Marriage

The family as such, with membership defined by kinship, depends for its survival on the marriage of its individual members. The rules governing marriage vary greatly; the notion of incest, however, is recognised in Africa as throughout the world, so a brother never marries his sister, nor a father his daughter, nor a mother her son. When the incest taboo covers the extended family with its far-reaching kinship network, exogamy is obligatory. There are, however, some tribes in which endogamy is the rule. As we pointed out at the beginning, Africa is a large and varied continent about which it is dangerous to generalise.

Since marriage is the means by which the family ensures its own survival, the organisation of a marriage is a very serious matter which concerns the whole family group. In African tradition, a marriage is first and foremost an alliance between two families, who arrange it in prescribed stages.

The first stage is *choosing the spouse*. The point to be noted here is that it is not the two people concerned who make the choice, although that does sometimes happen. Normally, for a first marriage, it is the man's family which selects the wife in accordance with certain criteria.

The second stage is *preliminary notification of their choice*. A delegation from the young man's family goes to 'knock on the door', as the Baoulés say, that is, to announce that the family intends to claim a particular girl for a particular son. Then follows a second visit, to make the actual demand for the girl. If the reply is favourable, there is a third visit, to make gifts of salt and drink, an act which betokens a certain measure of agreement between the two families.

Next comes the third stage, *the period of probation*. The whole village knows that the girl is to marry the young man, who consequently goes to her home every night. The girl will do various small jobs for her future in-laws, in particular for her mother-in-law, with whom she will occasionally go and work on their plot of land. For his part, the young man, with others of the same age, will go and work for the girl's family. Gradually, everyone comes to consider the couple as man and wife, though the girl is still living in her own home. This probationary period may last for years, and see children born.

The fourth stage in the marriage occurs when *the wife moves into her husband's home*. This used in the past to be a ceremonial occasion, with the wife escorted by women of her own age group and people showering her with the customary advice. The whole group would spend at least a week at the husband's home, and his family would make a point of honour of entertaining them as lavishly as possible. After the group left, the husband and wife really began their life together.

Their life together marks a further stage in the marriage, with the girl having left her own family and gone to live in another compound. She lives among her husband's family and bears children, but does not become a member of this family.[1]

When the married couple have lived together for a number of years, the husband may decide to take a second wife, even if he has no cause whatsoever to be dissatisfied with the first.

(b) Internal regulation and values

Within the large complex formed by the family, life and living are governed by precise rules. There is also an internal hierarchy, based on age; seniority is always deferred to and given precedence. In the patrilinear system, the oldest man is the head of the family. Even in the matrilinear system, where it is the oldest woman who has this status, her oldest brother acts in her stead, as women do not speak in assemblies even though it is common knowledge that no serious decisions are made without consulting them.

Another characteristic of the African family is the stress it lays on *harmonious relations*. The African sees discord as opening the door to trouble; as the proverb says, 'A cockroach cannot creep in to a wall with no cracks in it'. So disagreement must be vigilantly avoided, and every effort made to preserve good relations both within the family itself and between the family and the rest of the village. Dissension can lead to grave disorder, which may take the form of sickness. When that happens, a cure can be brought about by reconciliation.

Solidarity is another feature of the family, in times of joy as in times of suffering. But this does not mean that the family is turned in on itself; it expresses its solidarity through generosity and hospitality to others. Moreover, the extent of giving to and sharing with others is not governed only by what the family actually possesses, but quite frequently also by what others think it possesses. Wealth does not lie in riches and the storing up of riches, but in generous sharing with others.

(c) Rights and Duties of the Family

A final aspect of the family is that, like all its members, it has certain rights and duties. Each member knows what his or her individual rights and duties are, but rather than examine these in detail we prefer to concentrate on one area that in our view is all-important, the upbringing of the children.

Within the family the individual feels safe and integrated, and so provided he plays his proper part in it he can be assured of leading a full and balanced life, though his freedom as an individual will obviously be very limited.

The family's most important duty is the upbringing and education of its members, a process which begins well before birth and ends only at death. A pregnant woman is subjected to all sorts of prohibitions to ensure that her baby will be strong and healthy.

In the first years of its life, the baby develops very strong bonds with its mother, who is always in physical contact with it and suckles it on demand. In a sense, the period of gestation is not yet over.

When the child is weaned, the second stage in its upbringing begins, and now the whole family—uncles, aunts, brothers, sisters, grandparents—is involved. Any adult in the family is entitled to chastise a child who misbehaves. The whole village community shares in bringing it up. The child thus feels that he is supported, encouraged and protected by all those around him, and so learns how to integrate himself into his society.

All this may sound like an ideal state of affairs for a child. But a moment's thought about how hard it is to please just one or two people will suggest what difficulty a child may have in a society where he has to obey the 'whims' of countless adults!

To summarise, despite its diversity the African tradition of the family and family life contains a number of constant features: its extension, the definition of kinship, the slow and gradual process of marriage, polygamy and provisions for divorce; its inner hierarchy, the value it sets on harmonious relations, on solidarity, generosity and hospitality; and a system of upbringing that leads to a high degree of social integration. But it must be pointed out that the age-old patterns are changing: individual freedom has begun to appear within the family, and the transformation society is undergoing is affecting it too. A Christian living in this unstable world is faced with various problems, three of which, divorce, polygamy and marriage itself stand out in our view as requiring serious investigation.

2. PROBLEMS FACING A CHRISTIAN IN FAMILY LIFE

Before examining the difficulties an African Christian encounters in his family life, we must revert to the first missionaries' failure to try to understand African culture, a failure which in our view is one of the root causes of the present problems. When the evangelisation of Africa began, the missionaries made no attempt to study and understand the cultural universe of the people they wanted to convert; they were only concerned with winning as many souls as possible. As the superior of a missionary society puts it in John Munonye's novel *The Only Son*: 'In pursuit of that objective, I'm afraid we've got to be impatient with the culture of the people. There just isn't the time

D

to sort out first and label their customs as acceptable and unacceptable'.[2] In this rush to win souls, 'converts' were presented with alien norms and expected to accept and adapt to them and reject all their own culture, which was simply written off as bad. But as Robert Roenlandt says, 'Chronologically, culture always antedates the workings of faith in the human heart (. . .). The word of Jesus, the word which is at the heart of our faith, came into a pre-existing culture, but it did so as an answer to questions which that culture was raising, not as a bolt out of the blue. It is essential to know what these questions were in order to see the word of the Lord as a reply to them'.[3] For Africa, there has been no such preliminary study of the questions, and those of us who would be qualified to undertake it are so cut off from their culture when they finish their education that the problem is compounded. But if we are aware that for our faith in Jesus Christ to be rooted in our African culture we need a thorough knowledge of that culture, the first barrier has been overcome.

Christian moral teaching has had only a superficial influence on African tradition. True, there have been a few successes, in the sense that there are some Christian families which try to overcome the problems they meet, but they are surrounded by failure. For example, there are convinced Christians, Catholic action militants, who marry in church and then, a few years later, get a divorce. Some Christians, who were married in church, take other wives or keep a host of mistresses. Still others live together for years and are recognised by all as man and wife, but cannot take the ultimate step of a church wedding. Christ, our guide, unambiguously shows the way to those who would follow him. So why all these problems? That is what we shall be trying to elucidate in the light of African tradition.

(a) Common law marriage

Throughout the country marriage is undergoing a crisis, even in the villages, where the old customs are disappearing and young people are free to choose their partner. They are using this freedom by living together, while their parents take none of the customary steps to bring about a marriage. If, when they have had one or two children, they think they can go on living together, they ask their parents to make the traditional approaches. In many cases the marriage takes place in the traditional way and that is all. The Church is not brought into it; the idea of marrying in church never crosses their minds, any more than that of having a civil ceremony.

The African churches are performing a large number of baptisms, but very few weddings. Is this because people are deterred by the idea of the indissolubility of Christian marriage? The research which is being done in this area and examination of the question by the African episcopal conferences will help to solve the problem caused by having two separate sets of ceremony, common law weddings and Christian weddings, involving the same people. Given that in African tradition marriage is a slow and gradual process, the solution would perhaps lie in associating the Church with each stage of the arrangements made by the families, thereby giving a Christian character to common law marriages. Could the process of entry into marriage not be seen as comparable to that of entry into a religious order? The problem needs handling with care, but the African churches must not elude it.

(b) Polygamy

A second major problem in reconciling Christianity and African tradition is polygamy. Some see the African as polygamous by nature, and claim that polygamy is an African value comparable to family solidarity and hospitality. According to *Pro Mundi Vita*, which gives a survey of the question, in 78 per cent of the 742 tribes south of the Sahara polygamy is a moral value with an important role in the welfare of the tribe. It is presented in *Pro Mundi Vita* as a magical and multi-purpose cure, with the properties of the coil, the pill, tranquillisers and even the welfare state.

A short quotation from the text, giving some words of wisdom (!) from the lips of a pastor of the people of God, Mgr J. Njenga, the Catholic bishop of Eldoret in Kenya, will be revealing: 'In a polygamous family the convention is that there is a bond between two people, the husband and each of his wives (. . .). The husband feels deeply that each of his wives has a special relationship with him, that of husband and wife (. . .). This idea of marriage was accepted, respected religiously, and fulfilled (. . .). In any case, each of the wives has a monogamous relationship with her husband'.[4]

Faced with this defence of polygamy, which Africans in their search for authenticity are bending over backwards to present as an African value, there is just one question we can ask. Has anyone tried to find out what African women feel about polygamy? Has anyone tried to imagine what goes on in the heart and mind of a wife in a polygamous marriage when her husband is legally in the arms of another woman, her co-wife? Or to imagine the feelings of a woman who has spent her youth with a man who, though he is her own age, is now, quite lawfully, sleeping with girls young enough to be their own daughters, while she, her youth spent, and in all the anguish of the approaching menopause, has to sleep alone, with no-one to share her fears of the dark?

Is this justice? Why should the husband be legally entitled to variety and change of partners? What evidence is there for the idea that 'a woman would not sincerely feel that each of her husbands has a special relationship with her', to adapt Mgr Njenga's words.

Far be it from us to argue the feminist case; we want the old African traditions in which a wife loves and respects her husband to be observed and maintained. But we also want it to be realised, by everyone without exception, that the institution of polygamy is unjust in its very essence, and that it can only be tolerated as a second-best and no more, regardless of all the virtues attributed to it.

What man worth calling a man would like to find himself even for five minutes in the same position as co-wives, having, quite legally, to share with one or more other men the care and love of the same wife? One single quotation from the gospel should suffice to rouse awareness both of the problem and of its solution: 'Always treat others as you would like them to treat you: that is the Law and the prophets' (Matt. 7:12). These words of Christ are valid for all, for the old husband who took several wives before his conversion, for the child, for everyone whatever his chosen state in life.

(c) Divorce

With divorce, we reach an area where our traditional pattern of family life is in conflict with the specific teaching of Christ about marriage.

In Matthew 19:3-6 we read: ' "Is it lawful for a man to divorce his wife on any and every ground?" He asked in return, "Have you never read that the Creator made them from the beginning male and female?"; and he added, "For this reason a man shall leave his father and mother, and be made one with his wife; and the two shall become one flesh. It follows that they are no longer two individuals: they are one flesh. What God has joined together, man must not separate".' We find the same words in chapter 10 of Saint Mark's Gospel. Jesus' teaching on the indissolubility of marriage is unequivocal. The only question that can arise is when there actually is a marriage. As we saw earlier, in traditional African society marriage is a slow process which is bound up with the very process of living.

In the past, though divorce was provided for and accepted, it was very uncommon, as the families of the married couple would always find a way of reconciling the partners. But now it is the families which are causing trouble between them. The gospel says that 'a man shall leave his father and mother, and be made one with his wife; and the two shall become one flesh'. But it is simply not possible for an African, however educated and westernised he may be, and however strong his faith, to leave his father and mother and cleave to his wife. If one ever does so, then his family will take it as evidence that his wife has put a spell on him, and will go to any lengths to break up the marriage in order to recover 'its' son.

Christian discipleship requires a change of outlook and attitude. It is our task as Africans to find a way of reconciling the demands of Christianity with those of the family in our tradition, and so develop a specifically African form of Christian living.

To close this study, let us say quite simply that it is pointless to continue repeating that there has been no real meeting, based on a mutual exchange of ideas, between the traditional African view of the family and the Christian faith. What we have to do now is learn the lessons of the past and tackle the problems of today in order to prepare the way for a better future. Saint Matthew shows in his gospel that the Jews who followed Jesus were called on to transcend their own values, although they were those of the culture in which Jesus was born and spent his years on earth. Why should we African Christians not be called by the words of Jesus to do likewise? Clearly, before a whole way of thought can be changed, it must be fully known and understood. In African tradition the family has its own values which should not automatically be scorned. But we must not let our search for an authentically African Christianity blind us to the fact that our traditional values are not necessarily or automatically Christian. We must make them Christian.

When the bishops of the African churches use the freedom they have been given to select from our heritage such elements as will enable us to live both as Christians and as Africans, the guidance of the Holy Spirit will ensure that they make the best choice possible. African Christians will then no longer be constantly torn between their Christianity and their traditions, but will be able to live in inner harmony.

Translated by Ruth Murphy

Notes

1. Guerry pp. 46-47. Although she is referred to as a wife as soon as the young man's relations have been to ask for her, the marriage is not yet completed, and she retains some degree of independence even after moving into her husband's home.
2. Munonye p. 193.
3. Roenlandt pp. 29-37.
4. *Pro Mundi Vita* p. 19.

Bibliography

Déclaration du Symposium des Conférences épiscopales d'Afrique et de Madagascar (Nairobi 1978).
Directives pastorales de l'Episcopat sur la discipline des Sacrements (Abidjan 1969).
Erny P. *L'Enfant et son milieu en Afrique Noire* (Paris 1972).
Guerry V. *La Vie quotidienne dans un village baoulé* (Abidjan 1970).
Legrain M. *Mariage chrétien. Modèle unique?* (Paris 1978).

Message du Symposium des Conférences épiscopales d'Afrique et de Madagascar aux familles chrétiennes (Nairobi 1978).

Munonye J. *The Only Son* (London 1966).

Odi A. G. *Le Problème de l'éducation dans le roman africain de langue anglaise.* Thèse pour le Doctorat de 3 ème cycle (Montpellier 1977).

Pro Mundi Vita (Brussels 1976).

Roenlandt R. 'Culture et foi' *Telema* 17 (Jan. March 1979) 29-37.

Symposium des Conférences épiscopales d'Afrique et de Madagascar: vers l'indigénisation du rituel chrétien du mariage (Accra 1976).

Tardits C. *Porto-Novo: les nouvelles générations africaines entre leurs traditions et l'Occident* (Paris 1958).

Telema 1976, 4; 1978, 1; 1979, 1.

PART II

Philosophical Problems about Universality and Particularity

Bernard Quelquejeu

Diversity in Historical Moral Systems and a Criterion for Universality in Moral Judgment

THE NUMBER and variety of the specific moral systems by which human groups live is by now a well-established fact, attested by the convergent and complementary findings of ethnology, sociology, history and geography. The variety is obvious to the historian, whose task it is to study and familiarise himself not only with the evolution of moral concepts, ethical ideas and rules, but also with the history of morals, of moral practices themselves. It is no less obvious to the ethnologist or sociologist considering different societies and different cultures at a single period in history; they cannot fail to be struck by the immense diversity of actual moral systems, the ways in which societies decide the organisation of their community life, the division of property, the transmission of knowledge and skills, the exercise of power and cultural and religious expression. Since human beings have travelled and come in contact with societies other than their own, they have been forced to recognise the immense variety of actual moral responses which human groups have offered and still offer to the specific questions posed to them by individual existence and community life. The apparently irreducible diversity of the moralities by which human groups actually live is an unavoidable fact.

This acknowledged fact, at a very early date, posed extremely serious practical questions and, as a result, an inescapable theoretical question which philosophers have had to face ever since philosophy appeared and sprang into flower on the coasts of Greece. Difference in technical practices raises little question because techniques as such are not susceptible of any justification other than that of their efficacity. It is not the same with moral practices, which always include the assertion of a legitimation, since they involve an end. Let us make no mistake. To see in the diversity of moralities no more than a phenomenon which manifests the wealth of human potentialities is an abstract attitude; it neglects the inescapable question of knowing what provides the basis, the legitimation, of a particular morality, and leads to moral relativism, which in turn gives rise to moral indifferentism and scepticism. The practical attitude adopted from the beginning by human groups is quite different; the existence of a morality different from its own has always been felt by one group as a very serious threat, as a danger to its own survival as a group. History is filled with the sound and fury of wars of morality, like wars of religion, in which each side has tried, and still tries, to impose its own morality on others by force of arms. This simple statement indicates the seriousness of the practical questions raised by the existence in fact of different moralities and resolved for the most part by violence. Underlying these practical questions, a theoretical question makes its inescapable claim on the philosopher: Is there a justification for this historical, cultural and religious variety of particular moralities? This question immediately takes a different, prior, form: What is the basis for the legitimacy of a particular morality?

We could follow the evolution of this question through the whole history of philosophy since it was considered by Plato in his 'moral' dialogues (the *Crito*, the *Charmides*, the *Meno* and the *Laws*), then by Aristotle in his *Nichomachean Ethics*, down to today. In this long study we would have to stress the crucial contribution of Kant, whose achievement it was, in the *Foundations of the Metaphysics of Morals* and then in the *Critique of Practical Reason*, to have established, for the first time in its full rigour, the criterion of universality as the fundamental legitimation of the moral law. Is it possible in a few pages to give a brief account of this study of centuries without going into the differences which constitute the distinctiveness of the different philosophical systems? As always in such an enquiry, the crucial step is to choose the right starting point; the correctness of this choice determines, to a very large degree, the realism and the truth of the results obtained.

1. AT THE BEGINNING OF EVERY MORAL LIFE IS AN EDUCATIVE COMMUNITY

No-one invents morality. I mean that no-one embarks on it from zero. Before raising moral questions, before asking about the legitimacy and truth of morality, and before going on to a re-examination of a moral system, every human being already 'possesses' a morality. He or she already lives, more or less comfortably and more or less faithfully, by a system of morality, the one *in* which he or she was brought up.[1]

In the beginning, then, is education. More precisely, an education. Human beings are not born human; they have to become human, and for that education is indispensable—without it they will never become human. Proof of this has been provided by the cases of the 'wolf children', abandoned in the depths of a forest at the age of a few weeks and saved from certain death by being adopted by a family of wolves (or baboons, or leopards, etc.). Where they have been subsequently, at the age of five or six, returned to the human world, it has been found that the absence of human education during the crucial years of early infancy leaves gaps which cannot be filled and permanent handicaps in the subsequent acquisition of such specifically human characteristics as language, the ability to live in society, and moral sense.

To become a human being, the young offspring of woman thus needs to be educated, and this process always takes place in a family, a country, in an individual moral community. It is from that community that the young creature receives its morality, the morality which is recognised, lived and taught, the morality which governs conduct, defines attitudes, formulates what is permitted and what is forbidden, what is 'good' and what is 'bad'. But—and this is important—the individual does not at first regard the morality in which he or she is brought up as *one* morality among others, which may be equally valid, but as morality itself, the necessary morality. It is the morality which is 'obvious', which receives from all consciences (in particular those of parents, educators, sages, various figures of influence, perhaps religious authorities) the unconditional homage due to values which have assumed the character of the absolute. 'My' morality is morality itself, the only morality, the right one, the one of which it is obvious that it is right for everybody and about which no questions need be asked. Morality is obvious: everyone knows what they have to do because it is good and what must be avoided because it is bad. It is true that there are some moral problems, but they arise in relation to existing morality and within its framework. And of course there are figures recognised as qualified to resolve them, the elder, the sage, a particular competent person. The important thing is that people do not judge morality; they judge in terms of it, because it is obvious, 'natural'. In the beginning is moral certainty.

It should be added that this situation may remain stable, unchanged, for centuries. It has happened that societies have lived in conditions of great stability and near immobility, with no change or change so slow that it has not been noticed from one generation to the next. A combination of conditions exists such that the transmission of customs, models of behaviour and practical values takes place without raising questions: 'morality' continues to be taken for granted and certainty remains unshaken. Some so-called 'primitive' peoples and even some mountain valleys at previous periods of our own history before the arrival of the railway and roads have provided examples of such communities without perceptible change. True, individuals had 'moral problems', created by the greater or lesser difficulty they had in respecting all the imperatives of the dominant morality, but this morality remained, even for them, recognised as unchallenged and unchallengeable, 'obviously' untouchable.

2. ENTRY INTO HISTORICAL CHANGE AND ITS CONSEQUENCES

For us, for a long time now, things have ceased to be like this. A certain number of new factors has intervened, among which we may mention the huge expansion of knowledge, the progress of technology, which has brought new powers, the diversification and division of labour in society, the development of transport, and the rapid and widened transmission of information as a result of printing and then of telecommunications, etc. Under the influence of these factors our societies have emerged from immobility and have entered the age of social change, which has become more and more rapid and profound. Thanks to the possibility of cumulating knowledge, techniques, tools, and institutions, they have ceased to live in the cyclic and circular duration of nature, the medium of societies without history, and have entered social change, have entered history.

This change explodes within the dominant morality; it upsets, shatters, what was until this moment a peaceful moral certainty. One of the first effects of communication and transport is indeed to bring into relation—and very soon into conflict!—each ethical community with another, with several others. The community now discovers that there exist moralities other than its own, other ways of organising, and conferring meaning upon, work and its techniques, interpersonal relations, sexuality, authority and education. In the beginning was morality, and now we have the epoch-making discovery that this morality was only one morality among others, an individual, particular morality, and we find it, in the same instant, branded as uncertain, challengeable, doubtful.

The conflict between moralities, which arises in its full sharpness in the typical case of a prolonged encounter between two historical societies, appears most frequently in the more classical form of contradictions within a single morality. Two forms of behaviour, appealing to two different conceptions of the 'good' and governed by two contrary imperatives, make their appearance within the community and are offered together to the individual whom the community has the responsibility of enabling to live within it. The simultaneity of two contrary imperatives concerning a single course of action gives notice that the dominant morality has been shaken: it can no longer lay claim to obviousness, to the certainty of 'It goes without saying that one doesn't do that'. In contrast to a widely held opinion, therefore, it must be maintained that the appearance of cases of conscience is in the first place a bad sign for the morality by which a community lives. Their appearance announces the end of the dominant morality's claim to certainty or absoluteness.

In this way conflict between historical moralities reveals the possibility that any particular ethic can be undermined. It also reveals a harsh truth, which shatters many of the dreams and illusions which human beings are tempted to use to avoid a knowledge of their condition: there is no golden age of morality. This discovery, which accompanies the recognition of the incurable relativity of any historical morality, is a terrible wound which marks a person for ever by revealing to them their inescapable fragility, contingency and finitude.

This is not a pleasant or painless experience. The person who, not content with having, like everyone else, difficulties in following his or her morality and so having 'moral problems', now starts asking questions about that morality and so gives notice that they are no longer bound by the judgment of the dominant morality, which is precisely what they have challenged. Having rejected the claim of that morality to be obvious, they can only be regarded with extreme suspicion and intense reprobation by the upholders of 'obvious' morality. The questioners will be accused of breaking the consensus of their community, denounced as 'immoral' by those who continue to adhere to it without question. What they are doing is challenging the unconditional character of their historical morality, its 'sacredness'. They are defying the gods of the tribe, trampling underfoot the ideals of their educative community. They are traitors, iconoclasts: they must be removed, put to death. This was always the fate of moral innovators, of Socrates, Jesus and so many others.

3. TOWARDS THE PLEA FOR UNIVERSALITY

From this point, therefore, the individual in a modern society finds himself in an ethical situation which no longer has the beautiful simplicity enjoyed by a member of an ancient society, which would live by a ready made morality, one worked out in all its details and clearly prescribing a specific imperative for every kind of possible action. When the modern individual has to act he must, to a large extent, work out his own conduct: deliberation, moral judgment and practical decision-making often take on a complexity and uncertainty previously unknown.

A human being, we said, always starts by receiving the specific imperatives of his actions handed down from his educative community. What happens when he abandons his initial certainty and discovers that *the* morality he possessed is only *one* morality among others, an individual, specific morality? We could say that it is only then that he really embarks on moral debate, on thinking about morality—and soon about the very possibility of any morality. Because his own morality no longer offers him, directly, by itself, a solid foundation, his problem is to regain that lost certainty.

What quest, what demand, can push such a person towards an awareness of the *particularity* and contingency of his morality except those prompted by the *universality* of which he discovers himself to be, as a human being, the bearer? As soon as a person begins to question his particular morality, as soon as he begins to look for a new basis, a criterion which will allow him to verify the morality of his morality, he is, whether he knows it or not, responding to the need to go beyond that particularity, responding to the plea for the universal as the truth of his particularity, as the criterion of the practical truth of his particular action. He discovers that he is not only a member of a particular historical community—even though in fact he always remains such and can never break free—but is also under an obligation to come to terms with his membership of human universality, to respect, in himself and in others, what it is that constitutes being human, openness to the universal. Only in this way can individuals regain something of their certainty lost when their historical morality was challenged. As the bearer of this demand for universality which, as a criterion of morality, makes him a moral agent in the strict sense, the human being realises from this point that he has to submit every particular imperative of his moral practice to this criterion of universality. Any specific maxim for action, any decision, any moral practice which contradicts this criterion will be regarded as purely and simply immoral, that is to say, any rule which is opposed to the reciprocal and common exercise of reasonable liberty among human beings—which, in Kant's famous formula, cannot become a rule for any human being placed in the same conditions without reintroducing violence into human relations and, in the end, bringing about the immorality of the destruction of the weaker party.

Verifying the actual morality of the imperatives of one's own morality by means of this criterion of universality comes down in the end to applying to ethics the fundamental principle of non-contradiction. It is contradictory to demand for my particular case a rule of action which cannot be set up as a rule valid for all, a universal rule. Non-contradiction, yes, but only if we immediately add that, in practice, contradiction in morality is violence, war, the annihilation of others. Openness to human universality, in the strict sense, expresses a decision in principle to leave violence behind and live in the human land of mutual recognition, negotiation, the common expansion of liberties. In quite general terms, any action is good which issues from a free will freely exercised and which, in that act, accordingly respects the right of each person to free self-fulfilment. Any action is bad which is not in conformity with this universal openness and which, in some way infringing the essential right of every person freely to fulfil themselves, reintroduces violence into relations between human beings. The plea for universality is in the end nothing other than the utterly radical transcription on to the heart of personal freedom, of the prohibition 'Thou shalt not be thy brother's murderer.'

4. PARTICULAR IMPERATIVE AND UNIVERSAL RULE

This demand that the specific imperatives of morality should be subjected to verification by the criterion of universality does not entail the existence of an actual, complete universal morality. Such a deduction would be completely mistaken. To make it would mean, quite simply, denying the incurable contingency of human beings, the finitude of the human condition, abandoning the human realm. While it is true that human beings must hold themselves open to the universal, in their action they never cease to be particulars, subject to the unrepeatable uniqueness of the conditions of such action. Universal man does not exist; no more does universal morality. Only this or that man or woman, this individual historical community, really exists. To deny this historicity is to destroy human beings as they are, in the flesh, in their unbridgeable differences. That is why any actual morality, internalised in the individuals of a society thanks to education, is tied to the particular historical conditions of that educative community, which means that any real morality is particular and historical and will continue to be so. By the same token it too is subject to historical change. Any claim to seek to freeze historical morality in order to attribute to it the characteristics of permanence, absoluteness and eternity is a denial of this relative and historical condition of any actual morality. It means freezing and stopping it in the form it took at a certain period of its history. Human beings and society live. Morality must live.

But what are we to make of the idea that a morality can never escape from the conditions of its historicity and yet is, at the same time, called to be open to human universality—under pain of degenerating into violence? What are we to make of this inner complexity, of which at present we understand only that it is nothing other than the expression of the dual status of human beings, unique, needy and historical—and yet, as members of the human race, called to fulfil themselves freely and rationally? When he tries to find out how he should act and asks what imperative his action should obey to be 'good', historical man, living in a particular culture, never encounters abstract values, rules in the pure state. As a particular being and having to act in a situation which is likewise particular, he has to obey an imperative which particularises one or more rules in terms of the meanings of the factors involved as given by his culture. If one analyses them closely, one thus finds that every particular imperative transmitted by an ethical community is the transcription, carried out in function of its cultural meanings, of an abstract value of universal norm. To take an example, the (particular) imperative expressed in the prohibition of lending at interest is the result of such a transcription. A rule—not unjustly taking the property of another—is applied to the economic situation of the time, to its dominant mode of production, to the meaning of money in that culture. For centuries the transcription of the rule (not robbing others) in terms of the economic and cultural meaning of money resulted in the particular imperative: lending at interest is forbidden. As long as economic development (the artisanate, commerce, new industries, etc.) had not introduced profound changes in the meaning of money, this prohibition could be considered as a correct transcription of the prohibition of theft. A day came when the economic and cultural meaning of money—and perhaps also the economic position of the clerical Church—changed and it was necessary, in order to keep alive the rule about the property of others, to authorise lending at interest and so to change the particular imperative. That is what happens to morality when it is alive. As a result of social and historical change, it is obliged constantly to question the particular imperatives it imposes on consciences to verify that they are still the correct cultural transcriptions of the normative intention which makes human beings human. Nothing is more destructive of a moral conscience than forced conformity to an outdated imperative which no longer transmits the moral energy of which it should be the vehicle.

CONCLUSION

The considerations which have emerged in the course of this discussion bring home to us the simultaneous truth both of the variety of historical moral systems by which particular societies have in fact lived and of the plea for universality, the only firm foundation and criterion for the verification of morality. Imprisoning human societies in their historical particularity—the culturalist prejudice—results in depriving moral systems of their basis and their human legitimacy; it prevents us from understanding them as normative moral systems and reduces them to techniques of social organisation which happen to work. Conversely, refusing to accept as real any morality which is not universal and denying the ineradicable element of historical, cultural and religious particularity which each of them contains—the idealist prejudice—means preventing ourselves from allowing for the irreducible finitude of human beings and crushes humanity under the deadly requirement of a uniformity which denies differences. Both of these reductions in the end deny what is specific in moral life and moral principles.

This is the context in which we have to place the tradition of 'human rights' and, in particular, the *Universal Declaration* adopted by the United Nations on 10 December 1948. It is not, and would not claim to be, the establishment of a genuinely universal morality, but it is an irreplaceable formulation, of course open to improvement, of the general criteria which must be satisfied at present by the moral systems in force, in their geographical, national, ethnic and other diversity and according to their economic, juridical, social, civic, political and cultural solidity, if they are not to be destructive of the human dignity which it is their vocation to protect and promote.

After many centuries during which they have claimed the right to settle their moral differences by wars, human beings have today started to become aware of their fragility and their finitude. They know that they are irreducibly historical and that they are therefore situated, conditioned, by a whole series of particular, unique factors. They also know, however, that they begin true moral inquiry only by not accepting themselves as they find themselves given to themselves. They are indisputably first of all children with an upbringing, sexual beings, regional, national beings, social partners, and so on, but they are also—first of all—called to become human.

Translated by Francis McDonagh

Notes

1. In the preceding expressions and in several of those which follow, those familiar with the discussion will easily recognise the influence of Eric Weil's studies. His work, notably *Philosophie morale*, makes an invaluable contribution to the question studied here.

Enrique Dussel

One Ethic and Many Moralities?

AT THE end of this article—without any etymological or theoretical pretensions—I distinguish between *ethics* and *morals*. By ethics I mean a level of practical requirements valid for everyone in every historical situation. If world history forms a *single* totality, there is a *single* ethic. By *morals*, on the other hand, I mean the level specific to a particular historical system (Aztec, Inca, Egyptian, Chinese, Greek, feudal, European capitalist, etc.). As there is a plurality of particular historical totalities, and as there are different epochs in history, it is a historical and sociological fact that there are *many* different moralities. Faced with this *fact* of different moralities, the question is how—if at all—we can justify a *single* ethic valid for the whole of world history as the *omnitudo realitatis* of concrete human existence.

1. HEGEL'S ATTEMPT[1]

The Tübingen philosopher and theologian (1770-1831) was born a century after the triumph of the English bourgeoisie, and in his youth saw the bourgeoisie seize power in France. His life coincided with the spread of industrial capitalism. His theoretical work led, either consciously or unconsciously—this does not matter—to an ethical system which articulated and explained—and so justified—bourgeois morality. For this, he made use of the best of a long theoretical tradition which there is no space here to recount; we can only point to its fruits, its contributions to the development of thought.

As for Kant ('the root of evil')[2] and Schelling ('hence the universal need for sin and death as the real negation of particularity),[3] so also for Hegel, good consists in 'not upholding particularity as essential in the face of universality'.[4] In other words, evil is particularisation, taking the part for the whole, concentrating on the specific without daring to plunge into the universal: 'The finite immediacy of the individual subject . . . is first defined as nothingness and evil, and then (embarks on) the movement which consists in the negation of one's immediate natural determination . . . so as to come together with oneself in the pain of negativity and in this manner to know oneself as united to essence'.[5] Evil is someone who is and persists in being different, distinct, determinate, and who refuses to dissolve himself in 'the Same', the All, the Absolute of being—an act resembling Hindu *nirvana* or *gnosis*.

Hegel bases his consideration of the singleness of ethics and the plurality of morals in world history on this ontology of Totality. The plurality of morals comes effectively to

54

be found at the level of the degree of universality attaching to the 'moral code' of each people. The individual as particularity is taken up in and swallowed up by his country, whereas: 'Concrete ideas, the spirits of peoples, have their truth and definition in the concrete Idea, which as concrete Universality is the Spirit of the world'.[6] One should not forget that this 'Spirit' is the Holy Spirit in his *Philosophy of Religion*.

So, what is the relationship between the particular moralities of different peoples in history and the universal ethic of world history? Hegel explains: 'Since history is the configuration of the Spirit in the form of event . . .',[7] 'the people that receives such an element as a natural principle . . . is the dominant people at that period in world history. . . . Against the absolute right this people has as present bearer of the degree of development of the world Spirit, the spirit of other peoples *has no rights at all*.'[8] This means that the particularity of the moralities of different peoples is resolved on the level of a universal ethic through fetishisation of the morals of the dominant people at a given epoch of world history. In other words, a universal ethic is not found on the level of an abstraction valid for all peoples and all cultures, but is simply the particular morality of a people that as 'bearer' (*Träger* in the original) of the Spirit—and it bears the Spirit simply because it dominates the world in its time: domination becomes a manifestation of divinity—takes on in its own particularity the concrete universality of world history as a totality. And if we bear in mind that this people bears the Spirit in order that God may recognise himself in it and bring about the full realisation of his Return in it, then it will be seen that the universal ethic, the fetishisation of the morality of the dominant people, is the State religion.[9] The moralities of other peoples, 'like barbarians',[10] can find a place only 'round the throne (of the dominant people) as agents of its fulfilment, as witnesses and ornaments of its splendour'.[11]

Humanity can seldom have found a better theology of domination!

2. POST-HEGELIAN ATTEMPTS

Thanks to Schelling in his old age,[12] to Kierkegaard's critique of the fetishisation of Christianity,[13] to the Lutheran theologian Feuerbach's sensitive recall to christological principles,[14] and to many others, a whole generation rebelled against the idealist philosophy of Identity. Karl Marx (1818-1883) belonged to this generation, and the whole of his thought can be classed as ethical in intent. Really, from the 1844 writings to his death, he was dealing with just one theme: 'Thou shalt not steal!' If he can be criticised for anything, it is that this demand so obsessed him that it became the *leitmotiv* of his being, both practically and theoretically. The theme of the morality of particular systems and the requirements of a universal ethic forms the basis of his inquiries—a fact that often goes unnoticed by his supporters and detractors alike.

He analyses a given system, a specific totality, and its historical morality: that of capitalism. His conclusion is that the system as a totality, or political economy as its theoretical expression, behaves as a limitation denying, despising, not discovering or appreciating exteriority, otherness, other people: 'Political economy does not consider the unemployed worker, or the working man, in so far as they are *outside* the wage-earner relationship. . . . They are figures who *do not exist* for it, except as *for other people*, for the eyes . . . of the poorhouse warden; they are ghosts *excluded from its kingdom*'.[15]

The subject and the requirements of a universal ethic belong to the realm of the exteriority of the system and capitalist morality. The proprietor and the wage-earner are parts of capitalist morality but man '*as man*' and not only '*as worker*' falls outside the scope of the system.[16] *Man*, who also works, is really *nothing* to the capitalist system: 'The abstract existence of man as pure working man . . . can fall every day from its full nothingness to absolute nothingness, in his social non-existence which is his real non-existence'.[17]

In other words, and understanding this nothingness as the reality of *exteriority* for the morality of the system,[18] man—not as the wage-earner who enters into a contract, but as a free subject who can also be subject of *other systems* since his real and specific being (which is the *subject* of a universal ethic) is not exhausted by the abstract relationship of 'wage-earner'—this man has absolute (ethical) needs over and above the abstract (moral) needs of capitalism. Capitalism's moral demand is: 'Thou shalt not steal thy neighbour's private property', or: 'Thou shalt acquire thy riches by the sweat of thy brow'. But it immediately contradicts itself, since some (the owners of capital) have the right to take over the private property of others (their work, which is largely unpaid). Then morality and political economy part company and 'the fact that each sphere measures me by standards different from and opposed to those of the other, morality by one set, political economy by another, stems from the essence of man's alienation'.[19] Morality no longer judges structures; it becomes 'arbitrary, occasional, trivial, non-scientific'.[20] The only area common to both sets of standards is a set of individual requirements well-defined in advance: sexual behaviour, behaviour in relation to the laws of the country, etc. There are no longer any absolute ethical criteria valid for both abstract morality and political economy, whereas one function of a universal ethic would be to judge political economy from absolute human criteria. Therefore, 'the relationship between political economy and morality . . . when it is not just a deceptive appearance but considered *essential*, cannot be anything other than the relationship between economic laws and morality. . . . Political economy is then limited to expressing moral laws in its own way'.[21] So not only does Marx not deny a universal ethic, but he criticises the hypocrisy of splitting off an abstract, restricted morality opposed to a political economy immoral in its principles and its conclusions. What absolute criterion did he use to judge whether an action was ethical or not? It was this (space limits me to quoting from an early work, but it would not be difficult to find the same theme in works of 1857 or 1863): 'Work, the *vital activity* (author's italics), productive *life* itself, seems to man a means to satisfy a need. . . . Productive *life* is *life* in general. It is the *life* that creates *life*. The nature of the species is to be found in its *vital* activity . . . free, conscious activity, the nature of human *life*. . . . Man makes his *vital* activity the very object of his will and consciousness. He has conscious *vital* activity. This alone makes his activity free. Alienated work inverts the relationship.'[22] Good consists in the full realisation of *human* life ('feeling, thinking, looking, seeing, desiring, acting, loving. . . . Man's grasp of *human* reality, his behaviour in relation to the object, is the affirmation of *human* reality'),[23] which is an absolute principle of universal ethics. The very basis of bourgeois morality and the capitalist system is judged and found wanting in the name of this principle: 'Political economy, despite its outwardly harmless appearance, is a true moral science, the most moral of all the sciences.'[24]

Why is this? Because: 'With respect to the worker, who grasps nature through his work, this grasping becomes an objectivisation, his own activity becomes activity for another and *of another*; the life-force becomes a holocaust of life, producing an object for the benefit of an outside power'.[25] Or, to put it another way, work, man's feeling and *spiritual* activity,[26] is objectivised in the product[27] and happiness[28] is regained in consumption or satisfaction of needs. *Life* is objectiveness in the product. All production is either for oneself or for others; this 'for others' is a requirement of society and of human development. This is good: I produce for him and he produces for me. But if there is no reciprocity, if I go on producing 'for him' and he produces nothing for me, then there is a 'loss': 'Objectivisation as *loss* of the object and slavery. . . . Life lent to the object confronts it as something strange and hostile'.[29] The accumulation of this 'loss of life', this 'holocaust' to a new god is the effective *death* of the worker, since unconsumed products produced are a loss of life. This god, made up of so many deaths, is *dead* capital',[30] 'dead Mammon',[31] the fetish to which the blood of all the workers is sacrificed as 'profit';[32] it is the beast of the Apocalypse.[33]

So Marx implicitly derives a universal ethic from criticism of historical and specific moralities. What Hegel regarded as good (the rule of the dominant nation), here becomes evil: the fetish for which the blood of the wage-slave is spilt.

3. THE ABSOLUTE AND CONCRETE CRITERION OF ETHICS

Europe's discovery and experience of other worlds (Oriental, Asiatic and Latin American cultures, etc.), other ethical codes, the values, norms and virtues of other peoples, gave rise to various attempts to find a universal basis for ethics: Nietzsche's 'eternal return of *the Same*';[34] the timeless and universal validity of *values*, even though their hierarchy could change, best exemplified in Scheller's phenomenological axiology;[35] the viewpoint of linguistic philosophy;[36] Heidegger's ontological critique,[37] etc. One by one, however, the limitations of each system became apparent. Generally speaking, they were all returns to a Kantian, neo-Kantian or pre-dialectical approach: positivisms or neo-positivisms. This can be seen from some aspects[38] of the reply to the question: What is the *absolute criterion* on which an ethic valid for *every* given moral situation can be based?

The final basis of ethical conduct—'ethnicity'—(which should not be confused with its morality) would not seem to be the *law*. The law as norm in the form of legislation is a requirement that good (the *bonum, télos* or 'project') be done. And yet the moral law of any given system (whether positive or based on 'custom') can be unjust. This means it cannot be put forward as an absolute criterion. Even 'natural' law as an expression of human 'nature' is in need of a profound rethink. The Spanish Catholic philosopher Xavier Zubiri[39] has shown how the essence of human nature can be known from its results; these, however, will only be seen fully at the end of history, which means that, in effect, human essence comes to be known dialectically and progressively, but never completely. The same applies to the 'natural' law: law can only be a principle of the morality of a system, not an absolute criterion.

Values are in the same category.[40] The axiological schools' exaltation of values is no more than an idolising of mediation. Values are no more than the character *held* (not the essence) by mediation *as* mediation: i.e., a possibility is 'valid' to the extent that it is an actual or possible 'means' to an end. So it cannot be an absolute criterion but only a step on the way to one. Idolising values hides the basis, the project, the essence of the system. Surreptitiously, the axiologists are once more trying to impose the European view of man through mediations which they claim to be everlasting and universally valid.

The same can be said of *virtue*, particularly since Nietzsche's critique.[41] The medieval *vice* of avarice later became the *virtue* of saving. In the *ethos* of medieval nobility it was a sin and a vice to build up capital; in bourgeois and capitalist morality, the virtue of thrift is taught to children from an early age. This a real asceticism whose object of worship is Capital. What criterion can show whether a *custom* (*habitus* or *hexis*) is a vice or a virtue?

Good, the *bonum, télos* or 'project' (Heidegger's *Entwurf*, identified with *Sein* and 'potential being'), can equally be called into question when it is made the basis of a given historical system: was the *télos* or *finis* of the medieval order the same as that of the capitalist order? Can I know through its *content* a perfect human aim which can judge the finiteness, the evil, the determination of the 'projects' of these moralities? If there is a higher criterion by which I can judge the projects or *télos* which have operated in history, then these cannot be the ultimate basis of ethical discernment.

Emmanuel Levinas has shown[42] that the Totality, the established order or system of 'the Same', can find in itself only the basis of a given morality (Greek, Aztec, medieval, capitalist . . .), but not the starting point of an ethic valid in every human situation—which it must be if it is to contain an absolute criterion. He has rightly shown that the sphere of the exteriority of the Other is the source from which an absolute, trans-ontological, metaphysical ethic must originate.[43] But Levinas has been unable to work out a political ethic, because since this falls into the ambiguity of a new totalisation, ethics would give way to a new morality of war and oppression. Partly thanks to the Frankfurt School,[44] but due far more to the Latin American peoples' struggle for liberation, we have been forced to work out a concept that will not only question historical moral totalities, but also build up *'new' Utopian totalities* analogical to them which can be used by the liberated peoples.[45]

In all these cases, the absolute, yet specific, criterion—or imperative—of an ethic valid for every human situation, capable of judging every particular historical moral system, could be expressed in these words: 'Liberate the poor and the oppressed!' The medieval formulation, 'Do good and avoid evil', was correct but completely abstract, which enabled it to justify a moral system on the basis of the notion of 'good' held by the system *itself*. It was only a moral principle, not an ethical one. The good of the system is the good of the oppressor; so the oppressor can be morally good and yet ethically perverse. He can be a perfectly 'good' capitalist according to bourgeois morality, and an unjust man because he pays inadequate (though not illegal) wages by ethical standards.

The principle 'Liberate the poor and the oppressed!', on the other hand, is the rational (besides being intrinsically Christian and biblical) *critical* criterion *par excellence* and the only one that can at one and the same time both include the moral system and, by its very formulation, demonstrate the inner transcendence and ethical exteriority of a future system, Utopian in its positivity and realism. In this concept, the 'poor' or oppressed include: (*a*) a totality in the form of an existing moral system; (*b*) an oppressor who is the subject of wrong actions; (*c*) a just man—at least in relation to the oppressor—unjustly treated. 'Liberate' includes: (*d*) taking account of the mechanisms of the established moral totality; (*e*) the ethical duty to take these mechanisms apart; (*f*) the need to build the way out of the system and the further duty of building a new system (still unsituated: Utopian) in which the oppressed of yesterday will be the citizen in the just morality of today.

This is an *ethical* requirement. It is ethical because it is trans-moral, trans-systemic, based on the exteriority of the Other, the poor, the oppressed. On the basis of the Other, and the *affirmation* of the Other (an *analectic* moment in the dialectic historical process) we can proceed to the *negation of his negation* in the system.

'Liberate the poor!' also has a *material*, fleshy content that can be grasped. It is a matter of feeding the hungry, clothing the naked, housing the stranger. As a requirement it is productive (giving bread: a product to be consumed), practical (with regard to the other), and economic (in respect of the historical structures of systems of oppression which have to be negated and the Utopian systems that have to be built up). It is a criterion that assumes the totality of the materialness of the *flesh* (*sárx, basar*), and the dialectical opposition to and overcoming of the plurality of moral systems on the basis of the requirements of a *transcendental, absolute* and yet concrete ethic—every historical system has had its oppressed!—because it is indissolubly linked to the mystery of human freedom.[46]

4. AN ESCHATOLOGICAL AND CRITICAL ETHIC

Historical moral systems inevitably 'close in' in the period of their decadence (the period Spengler called 'civilised'), when the creative *pathos* of their founders (Joan of

Arc, George Washington) gives way to empires (the Caesar, the protagonists of more and more arms to El Salvador) and the persecution and death of the Roman circuses. This is the totalised Totality of 'the Same'. In these periods—and the present is one of them—it is essential to have an absolute, trans-systemic, trans-moral criterion, going beyond being, good, the law, values, the virtue *of the system*. It is needed not only—this is secondary—as a theoretical explanation for, but primarily as a historical justification of the ethical legitimacy of the liberating actions of the heroes the system condemns as immoral, tortures in its prisons and murders as the 'dregs of humanity'.

An ethic that will clarify the absolute criterion by which non-ethical moralities can be judged thus becomes a strategic necessity for the politics of liberation itself. It is the theoretical justification of the supreme dignity of the acts of its martyrs and heroes, and, by destroying 'good consciousness', shows up the fetishistic perversity of the existing, triumphalist moralities of the dominant systems.

In order to be able to forgive the soldiers who were torturing him, as Jesus did, he had to see very clearly that they were 'good' by the standards of 'their' Roman morality, and so unable to discover for themselves (the *blindness* characteristic of the ideological moral conscience of the dominator) the absolute—but always concrete in the here and now—requirements of a Utopian ethic of liberation by virtue of whose absolute criterion Jesus could face death in peace. He knew that his death, that of a bandit or outcast from the ruling moral system, was legal praxis for the future morality of a juster system. But even the legality of a future historical moral system could be judged by the absolute criterion of the ethic: 'Liberate the poor and the oppressed!' Even this future moral system, being historical, could and should be judged from the standpoint of the radical transcendentality of the Other, the poor, the oppressed. The transcendentality of the ethic thus exists on the eschatological level: it can also judge every historical future, just as the concepts of liberation and poor include the dimensions of transcendentality, exteriority and eschatology. *The negated life of the poor always judges death as an evil.*

Translated by Paul Burns

Notes

1. Hegel's morality is contained in *Grundlinien der Philosophie des Rechts* (1821), and paras. 483-552 of the *Enzyklopaedie* (1817). In this context, see K. H. Ilting *G. W. F. Hegel, Vorlesungen über Rechtsphilosophie 1818-31* (Munich, vol. I, 1973); F. Rosenzweig *Hegel und der Staat* (Munich 1920); G. Lukacs *Der Junge Hegel* (Berlin 1954); E. Weil *Hegel et l'Etat* (Paris 1950); etc. Hegel concerned himself with the subject from his earliest writings, esp. *System der Sittlichkeit* (1802). For convenience, I quote from the *Werke*, vols. I-XX (Frankfurt 1969-71).

2. *Die Religion innerhalb der Grenzen der blossen Vernunft* (1793), B 39, A 36, n. 1; cf B 32, A 29ff.

3. *Über das Wesen der menschlichen Freiheit* in *Werke*, VII, p. 382. These are the Greek and neo-Platonic themes, Buddhist and Rig-Veda ones, passing through Bruno and Boehme.

4. *Rechtsphilosophie* § 129, in vol. 7, p. 262.

5. *Enzyklopaedie* § 570, in vol. 10, p. 376. This is again the great Indo-European theme and so Hegel refers to Krishna (p. 383), the Persian mystics, Djadal-Ud-Rumi: 'I have seen the One everywhere', and the Bhagavad-Ghita.

6. *Rechtsphilosophie* § 352, p. 508.

7. *Ibid.* § 346, p. 505.

8. *Ibid.* §347, pp. 505-506.

9. 'Religion and the basis of the State are one and the same thing, identical in themselves and for themselves' (*Phil. der Rel.* I, C, III, in vol. 16, p. 236.

10. *Rechtsphil.* § 351, p. 508.

11. *Ibid.* §352, p. 508.

12. Esp. the Berlin lectures of 1841 and *Philosophie der Mythologie* (begun in 1820) and *Philosophie der Offenbarung* (begun in 1827).

13. See *Post-scriptum* (Paris 1941); see K. Löwith *Von Hegel zu Nietzsche* (Stuttgart 1964).

14. Remember *Grundsätze der Philosophie der Zukunft* (1843) (Frankfurt 1967), with its famous § 62: 'The true dialectic is not the monologue of the solitary thinker with himself, but the I-thou dialogue' (p. 111).

15. *MSS of '44* in *Karl Marx Frühe Schriften* I (Darmstadt 1962), p. 576: 'Gespenster ausserhalb ihres Reiches'.

16. *Ibid.:* 'As soon then, as Capital wishes, the worker ceases to exist, he ceases to exist in himself; he has no work and therefore no pay, and since he has no existence as a person (*als Mensch*) but only as a worker, he might as well be buried, or let himself starve to death'.

17. *Ibid.*, p. 578.

18. Remember that 'nothing' means precisely 'beyond' the system. St John of the Cross experienced the exteriority of the world as 'nothing' when he wrote in *The Ascent of Mount Carmel:* 'After everything: nothing'.

19. *Ibid.*, p. 614.

20. *Ibid.*, p. 615.

21. *Ibid.*, pp. 614-615.

22. *Ibid.*, p. 567.

23. *Ibid.*, p. 598.

24. *Ibid.*, p. 612.

25. *Ibid.*, pp. 574-575.

26. Marx was very far from either common or cosmological materialism when he wrote: 'the worker does not expend free physical and spiritual (*geistige*) energy, but mortifies his body and ruins his spirit (*Geist*) (*ibid.*, p. 564).

27. 'After food, man's two greatest needs are clothing and shelter' (*Ibid.*, p. 548). Compare Matt. 25:35-6: 'For I was hungry and you gave me food, . . . I was a stranger and you welcomed me, I was naked and you clothed me'.

28. 'A society in which the majority are suffering is not a happy one . . . and the aim of Political Economy is the unhappiness of society' (*ibid.*, pp. 515-516).

29. *Ibid.*, p. 561.

30. *Ibid.*, p. 512: 'tote Kapital'.

31. *Ibid.*, '. . . toten Mammons'.

32. *Ibid.*

33. One of the favourite themes of *Das Kapital* is the metaphor from the Apocalypse of 'the chosen people bearing *on their foreheads* the message that they belonged to Jahweh; the division of labour stamps *on the forehead* of the industrial worker the mark of his owner: Capital'. See F. Hinkelammert *Las armas ideológicas de la muerte* (San José, Costa Rica 1977) pp. 26ff.

34. Nietzsche, who was an implacable moral critic, ended up by making an apology for the warrior and dominating *ethos* of the primitive Germanic invaders of Europe.

35. See *Der Formalismus in der Ethik*, in *Gesammelte Werke* II (Berne 1954).

36. See G. Moore *Principia Ethica* (Cambridge 1903). Also the ethical works of Ayer, Wittgenstein, etc.

37. Heidegger puts forward a genuine 'ontological ethic' against the subjective idealism of Sartre in the 'Letter on Humanism', in which he is equally critical of axiological ethics.

38. For all this, see my *Para una ética de la liberación* (I-II, Buenos Aires 1973; III, Mexico 1977; IV-V, Bogotá 1979-80).

39. See *Sobre la esencia* (Madrid 1963).

40. See my *Etica* (n. 38 *supra*), I, ch. 2, § 7, pp. 70ff. 'Values' cannot be the basis but only a stage in the process.

41. Esp. in *Zur Genealogie der Moral* and *Jenseits von Gut und Böse* (see *Etica*, *op. cit.*, II, pp. 82ff).

42. Cf. *Totalité et infini* (The Hague 1974).

43. I have given a summary explanation of this point in *Filosofía de la Liberación* (Bogota 1980), pp. 54ff.

44. See H. Marcuse *One-Dimensional Man* (Boston 1964), which had a great influence on the critical philosophy of Adorno, Habermas, etc.

45. The subject of Vol. I of *Ética*, cited in note 38.

46. This is a subject of which various Christian and Jewish writers such as Blondel, Zubiri, Bergson, Buber, Rosenzweig, etc. have explored different aspects.

PART III

Theological Solutions to the Problem of Uniformity, Universality and Pluralism

Josef Blank

Unity and Plurality in New Testament Ethics

1. THE PROBLEM OF UNITY IN PLURALITY

IT APPEARS that theological development also has its times and its rhythms and that now the pendulum is swinging back on this problem. Recently there was much discussion of the problem of theological pluralism and its justification[1] but now the question is again being asked as to what is enduringly common and uniform among all the plurality. This does not mean that pluralism in theology and the Church is in any way false or finished. There are good reasons for pluralism in theology today. It is a necessity both from the theoretical scientific and the historical sociological points of view. There is no virtue in denying it for the sake of outward 'uniformity' or 'unanimity' of doctrine. However, it is also important to seek for what is held in common amid the plurality to make plain that plurality is not a loose, optional association of arbitrary and completely heterogenous assumptions and opinions, but the manifold presentation and expression of what is in itself the 'one single reason for the Christian faith'. The task is to rethink the ancient problem of the relationship between unity and multiplicity.

The New Testament texts present this problem in an acute form,[2] because they do not offer a closed system but are texts with very different aims, theological conceptions and modes of thought. The New Testament texts also have different historical and socio-cultural backgrounds, as can be seen very plainly from, e.g., the four gospels. The social context in which Jesus' message was planted had a much stronger influence on its final written account, as we have it today, than we previously dared to believe. Modern study of New Testament texts, as practised by the 'theology of liberation' can give us a vivid impression of what a living process of reception of the Christian message looks like and what it must have looked like at the beginning. We can also see unmistakeably how in the course of time firm trends and particular standards crystallised out of it, and how these were then given recognition by the Church and led to a certain view held by the whole Church of the 'normal Christian'.

2. 'ITINERANT RADICALISM' AND 'LOVE PATRIARCHALISM'

Recently Gert Theissen, in particular, has produced several works on the problem of a 'sociology of primitive Christianity'[3] and noted the fundamental changes in the social structure of the early Christian movement.

On the one hand there was the 'itinerant radicalism',[4] first of all Jesus himself and his movement, then the disciples and wandering missionaries who emerged from this movement. This was chiefly documented in the traditions of the Logia source Q. Theissen lists the following as important points about the ethos of this itinerant radicalism:

(a) Jesus' words support an *ethos of homelessness*. 'Call to discipleship means: give up *stabilitas loci*'.[5]
(b) The Logia also support an anti-family ethos. 'The giving up of *stabilitas loci* includes the breaking off of family relationships.'[6]
(c) A further, connected, characteristic is the critique of wealth and possessions.

From this Theissen concludes: 'The ethical radicalism of the tradition of the word is itinerant radicalism. It can only be practised and passed on under extreme living conditions. Only one who is released from the world's daily ties, one who has abandoned home and hearth, wife and child . . . can truly practise and preach renunciation of home, family and possessions. Only under these conditions can such ethical doctrines be preached without losing credibility.'[7]

However, the primitive community in Jerusalem, which arose after the first Easter, spread into predominantly Hellenistic communities, particularly those founded by the Pauline missions, and the model of 'itinerant radicalism' was faced with a very different situation. These communities were mainly urban, in a big city environment in fact, if we think of metropolises like Antioch upon Orontes, Ephesus, Corinth, Alexandria and Rome, with their populations in the hundred thousands. Theissen uses the example of the community in Corinth to show that in this new, urban social situation, a radical re-direction of the Christian ethos became necessary.[8] The Hellenistic communities represent an evolved form of development of primitive Christianity. The cause was the passage of Christianity from the predominantly rural structure of Palestine to the urban Hellenistic culture of the Mediterranean. 'The history of early Christianity was thus determined by a profound social change even in the first generation. Important socio-cultural and socio-economic factors changed, through a process of Hellenisation, urbanisation and a rise into higher social classes.'[9] Jesus' itinerant radicalism in its original form became no longer practicable. There was no place for the ethical radicalism of the Jesus-tradition in the Pauline communities. So, according to Theissen there arose in the Pauline communities 'an ethos clearly distinct from the Synoptic tradition, the ethos of loving patriarchy, as we see especially evident in the Deutero-Pauline and Pastoral texts, although already present in Paul. . . .'[10]

This *loving patriarchy* takes social class distinctions for granted, although of course softening them through the duty to show consideration to the socially weak. 'Christian brotherliness,' says Theissen, 'could probably have been put into practice more radically in socially homogenous groups. But that is much easier to do than to practise brotherliness in communities with sharp social differences. Here early Christian loving patriarchy offered a realistic solution.'[11] This loving patriarchy as a new pattern for forming and controlling social relations as opposed to the society of antiquity had far-reaching significance for the whole society. Thus far Theissen.

3. ESCHATOLOGY AND SOCIAL STRUCTURES

Theissen's views are highly plausible and, taken together with other points of view, offer important help in the understanding of a whole series of problems in New Testament ethics.

One of these problems is *the eschatological motivation of the radicalism in Jesus' preaching*, which can only be understood in connection with the prophetic proclamation of the nearness of the kingdom of God and his reign.[12] Itinerant radicalism must therefore not be seen in isolation. It is the life-style corresponding to the proclamation of God's reign to all Israel. In fact this life-style is not wholly the result of the mainly peasant social structure in Galilee; important though this was, it had no necessary causal connection. The main reason for the itinerant radical life-style was the fact that the message of the imminence of God's reign had to be spread throughout Israel as quickly and widely as possible. The proclamation of the message of final salvation required, because of its urgency, a corresponding mobility in its chosen messengers. The term 'itinerant radicalism' was entirely appropriate for this process.

These demands, which can most probably be described as 'Jesus' ethics',[13] are closely connected with Jesus' proclamation of the kingdom. This raises the problem of the relationship between eschatology and ethics. Jesus proclaimed God's reign as God's coming reign of *salvation*. God's will is understood as overpowering love, which is endlessly greater than all human expectation and understanding, and which gives salvation, life and a limitlessly positive meaning to existence. Freedom and salvation guarantee and also summon people to surrender themselves totally to this eschatological understanding of life. 'Conversion', 'repentance'—*metanoia*—in this context means not only renouncing our own evil past and repenting it, but first and foremost the gift of new life, which makes the ethical reorientation of life possible. This is clearly illustrated in the parable of the 'unmerciful servant' (Matt. 18:23-35). The Lord overlooks the whole debt of his heavily indebted servant, ten thousand talents, which should have made him prepared to treat his fellow servant, who only owed him the ridiculously small sum of a hundred denarii, with similar kindness. But the servant is not capable of doing this. God is the forgiver and giver, but his gift is meant to call forth a response in the receiver and make him behave similarly. The point of the commandment to love our enemies is *human imitation of God*. 'You, therefore, must be perfect, as your heavenly father is perfect' (Matt. 5:48); or 'Be merciful, even as your Father is merciful', in Luke's version. The gift of God's reign is thus the beginning and motivation for a fundamental change in humans, in which a new way of behaving will be a 'fruit' of the new life.

The individual demands have as their aim the freeing of people from false ties—from the individual 'I' together with all that makes up this 'I' in its narrower and broader circle, especially 'possessions' and the corresponding 'possessor behaviour', 'having' (as E. Fromms calls it today). To make them available for the cause of God's reign and of course, therefore, for their fellows. To show them new possibilities of knowing and doing God's will. The main point is to open up the whole area of common human life in all its complexity and multiplicity as the domain of God's will.[14] The 'neighbour' or 'companion' I meet today in today's particular situation decides what God's will is here and now for me/us. In the conflict between the law and actual human need Jesus always chooses the latter and every law must be judged accordingly!

It seems fairly certain to me that Jesus, in contrast to the scribes, radically simplified discussion of God's will.[15] Jesus was clearly interested in the 'broad lines' and not casuistry. But this liberating sweep into the big issue, the surrender to the 'one thing necessary'—God's reign—can only be understood in terms of eschatological enthusiasm, which marked all Jesus' thinking and acting. Schweitzer was basically right to speak here of 'interim ethics'.[16] For it is true that there are only ethics until God's kingdom comes, and secondly, that in this eschatological context ethics can always only be seen as a 'provisional, temporary solution', a 'way', a denial therefore that human action can ever bring about a definitive state of salvation. The 'eschatological reservation' is not a theological mental restriction as such, although it sometimes appears to be one. It manifests itself in ethics as an unbridgeable gap in the actual history of human actions. *The gift and grace character of God's reign is meta-ethical and transcends the ethical*; but *precisely because this is the case it constitutes the ethical as the domain of human freedom and its realisation in love.* Ethics would do well to become aware of this difference again. Christian action in one sense always remains 'Samaritan service' and fragmentary. It does not need to give itself the appearance of absolute perfection. It must not correspond to the idealistic theory of behaviour or to legal formalism either. Thus it is free to cope with the present and its particular needs, free to act responsibly in any particular historical situation.

In any case it would always be difficult to put into practice this eschatologically orientated radicalism in communities or groups which were much less committed, or who had not the freedom or who lived in very different circumstances. We can clearly feel the anxiety about this in the Synoptic Gospels and also in Paul.

An important background to New Testament ethics is the early Christian struggle with the Jewish Torah and its validity. Jesus himself fully recognised God's revealed will in the Jewish Torah,[17] but in his interpretation of the Torah he quite clearly put new emphases and priorities, which showed a different basic tendency to that of the Torah interpretation of the Jewish Rabbis. Apparently, he regarded the whole area of cultic purity, which made it so difficult for the 'man from the country' to be legally pious, as more or less indifferent (see Mark 7:1-23; Matt 15:1-20), and he regarded only the ethical commandments as important (see Mark 10:17-19). This tendency continued among the post-Easter community, especially among the group of 'Hellenists' (see Acts 6 and 7), and was finally clarified in Pauline theology as 'justification by faith alone and not by the works of the law'. For the Jesus community the Jesus Halacha took the place of the Moses Halacha.

In the Gospel of Mark the problem of Torah piety practically no longer exists. The 'ethical chapter', Mark 10, handles the themes of divorce (Mark 10:2-12), 'becoming like children' (Mark 10:13-16), the example of the rich young man (Mark 10:17-22) and the warning against the dangers of wealth (Mark 10:23-27). The dispute about the tribute (Mark 12:13-17) illustrates the early Christian attitude to the State,[18] and the double commandment to love God and our neighbours (Mark 12:28-34) is intended as an all-embracing summing up of the Christian life. And this is the limit of the Gospel of Mark's ethical content. We may conclude which ethical contents were important for the Christian community of Mark.

In Matthew, on the other hand, discussion with the Jewish-Pharisaic Torah piety plays a very important part. In the Sermon on the Mount—a speech composition by Matthew—it is consciously contrasted with the new Messianic teaching of Jesus to his disciples. Matthew's Gospel stands for an open Jewish Christian tradition, which stresses above all the *meaning of Jesus' behaviour* and attaches particular value to it. Doing God's will in Jesus' sense is at least as important here as confessing him to be God's Son and the Messiah. As F. Mussner, in particular, has shown, Matthew's Gospel and the Epistle of James are quite close,[19] and they both agree that faith without works is dead (see James 2:14-17; Matt. 7:21-23). This line is continued in the *Didache*. Matthew took over much from the Jewish-Pharisaic tradition, especially the tradition of 'good works'.[20] He sees the cultic purity scriptures as basically superannuated, but leaves their fulfilment a matter of choice, while stressing the clear priority of love and mercy over the cult (see Matt. 23). The concept of 'mercy' as a Christian virtue comes very high with him (see Matt. 5:7; 6:14f; 18:21-2, 23-35). We note that this most systematic of the evangelists consciously uses the catechesis of the disciples, as a real 'school', probably in the closest possible connection between teaching and community practice. Matthew probably also drew his *great interest in the realisability of Jesus' sayings* from the Jewish-Pharisaic tradition.

Things are different again in *Luke's Gospel*, which lays the most stress on the social-ethical impulse. There are no more discussions with Jewish Torah piety. For Luke these belong to the past and are no longer of interest to his pagan Christian community. Therefore Luke, and this is a notable and greatly undervalued contribution from a Hellenistically educated man, draws a picture of Jesus with particular emphasis on the 'friend of publicans and sinners, the outcast, the poor, the humble and meek. He could be described as the inventor of the 'social gospel'. Luke not only offers a courageous alternative to the classical ideal of 'kalokagathia' and stoic 'ataraxia' and egocentric 'eleutheria', but a revolution in antiquity's whole hierarchy of values. It is the outcast, the despised and the poor, who in Luke include women, to whom God offers all his love in Jesus. Nowhere else is wealth seen as the great evil as clearly as in Luke. Only in him do we find the term 'unjust Mammon', which can be used to make friends by sharing it with the poor (see Luke 16:9). According to Luke there should be a free community of goods in the Christian community (see Acts 2:44f; 4:32; 5:1-11).

From these few examples, we can see how the early Christian ethos adapted itself to new situations and needs by new interpretations of Jesus' sayings. Very soon a broad reception was given to common ethical norms of the ancient world. Paul himself recommended the Phillippians to do everything that was true, honourable, just, lovely and gracious, everything that counted as *aretē*, as virtue (Phil. 4:8). He recommended them to hold on to the commonly recognised ancient virtues. This begins the process of the continuous dialogue between genuinely Christian New Testament modes of behaviour and virtues and the morality current in the society of the time.[21] This process of mutual influence on the one hand and critical conflict on the other seems to me as least as important in the understanding of Christian ethics as in the history of dogma. Up till now it has been very little researched, although this must be one of the chief causes of the necessary pluralism. It would be extremely useful to follow this throughout the New Testament, but space does not alllow us to do it here.

4. THE COMMANDMENT TO LOVE AS THE 'BOND OF PERFECTION' (COL. 3:14)

The early Christian tradition recognised fairly unanimously the commandment to love as the summing up of 'Jesus' ethics'.[22] The chief witness to this is Paul. He never quotes the double commandment to love God and our neighbour, but always only the commandment to love our neighbour. 'Concerning love of the brethren you have no need to have anyone write to you, for you yourselves have been taught by God to love one another.' (1 Thess. 4:9) Paul shows us that the 'chief commandment to love' had a central place in the early Christian catechesis. He himself learnt it in the tradition of the community. For him this commandment is the 'fulfilment of the law' (Gal. 5:14; Rom. 13:8-10). According to 1 Cor. 13, the 'great hymn of love', love is the 'greatest' of the gifts that Paul can name, the reality without which everything else is worth nothing. And here too love is described in its common everyday form as practical love of our neighbour. It is no accident that the literary form of 1 Cor. 13 is a hymn.

The well-known form of the double commandment to love God and our neighbour (Mark 12:28-34; Matt. 22:36-40; see Luke 10:25-28 and the parable of the Good Samaritan, Luke 10:29-37) probably does not derive from Jesus himself in the form that we have it.[23] However, there can be no doubt that Jesus gave the decisive impetus to the concentration of all human 'religion' and 'ethics' in this double commandment. In the tradition of John 'love one another' (John 13:34) is called Jesus' 'new commandment', more important than any other. Apart from this commandment there are no other ethical sayings in John, although he often speaks of 'the commandments' in the plural. The First Epistle of John, as Augustine noticed, speaks mainly about love—'locutus est multa, et prope omnia de caritate'[24]—and gives this new commandment and the word 'love' a matchless theological deepening, without in any way lessening the practical character of actually being and doing for others. (see 1 John 3:11-18). Although we cannot develop this theme further here, we can see the commandment to love provides the fundamental unity in New Testament ethics and a continuity which allows us to say that *it is the centre of Christian ethics*, which binds together the very different ethical ideas in the New Testament, in content as well as in form. This is even more noticeable, when we find yet other ethical ideas put forward by the 'Apostolic Fathers', which nevertheless still concur with the notion of Agape.

5. IN CONCLUSION

If we were to draw a general conclusion from the above remarks, we could say that basically there is no such thing, according to the New Testament, as a 'Christian ethics' as a firmly established 'system'. The task is always to confront Jesus' ethical sayings and those of the New Testament traditions/authors with changing socio-cultural circumstances and to put them in practice. However, this did not mean merely externally adapting the Christian way to a given culture. Christianity always became ethically effective by breaking open particular cultural traditions and critically altering them. Perhaps, particularly in the West with its traditions of domination, this should have been done much more radically. In any case the critique of given traditions, especially the Roman-Latin tradition in the Catholic Church, is a constant task for New Testament ethics. Here too salvation is at stake, the salvation and healing of human beings towards greater humanity.

Translated by Dinah Livingstone

Notes

1. For the whole problem see D. Tracy *Blessed Rage for Order. The New Pluralism in Theology* (New York 1975). *Concilium* 115, 5/1978 'Doing Theology in New Places'.
2. See A. Stock *Einheit des Neuen Testaments* (Zurich-Einsiedeln-Cologne 1969).
3. G. Theissen *Studien zur Soziologie des Urchristentums* (Tübingen 1979).
4. Theissen *Soziologie* pp. 79-105.
5. Theissen *Soziologie* p. 83.
6. Theissen *Soziologie* p. 85.
7. Theissen *Soziologie* p. 86.
8. 'Soziale Schichtung in der korinthischen Gemeinde. Ein Beitrag zur Soziologie des hellenistichen Urchristentums' *Soziologie* 231-271; 'Die Starken und Schwachen in Korinth, Soziologische Analyse eines theologischen Streites' *Soziologie* 272-289.
9. Theissen *Soziologie* p. 268.
10. Theissen *Soziologie* p. 268.
11. Theissen *Soziologie* p. 269.
12. R. Schnackenburg *Gottes Herrschaft und Reich. Eine biblische theologische studie* (Frieburg in Breisgau [1]1959); K. L. Schmidt 'βασιλεία, Die βασιλεία Gottes' THWNT, pp. 582-592; J. Jeremias *Neutestamentliche Theologie I: Die Verkündigung Jesu* (Gütersloh 1971) pp. 99-110; P. Hoffman & V. Eid 'Jesus von Nazareth und eine christliche Moral' QD 66, (Freiburg-Basel-Vienna 1975) 27-82; H. Merklein 'Die Gottesherrschaft als Handlungsprinzip. Untersuchung zur Ethik Jesu', fzb (Würzburg 1978).

13. See Hoffman-Eid 'Jesus von Nazareth und eine christliche Moral'; Merklein 'Die Gottesherrschaft als Handlungsprinzip'; R. Schnackenburg *Die sittliche Botschaft des Neuen Testaments* (Munich [2]1962); H. Preisker *Das Ethos des Neuen Testaments* (Gütersloh 1949); H. -D. Wendland *Ethik des Neuen Testaments. Grundrisse zum NT 4* (Göttingen 1970).

14. J. Blank 'Die Auslegung des Willen Gottes im Neuen Testament' in *Zum Thema: Wille Gottes* Denzler-Beck-Blank-Lang-Kuhnle (Stuttgart 1973) 83-114, esp. 97.

15. See J. Blank 'Lernprozesse im Jüngerkreis Jesu' ThQ 158 (1978) 163-177.

16. For the idea and the problem of 'interim ethics' see A. Schweitzer, *Das Messianitäts- und Leidensgeheimnis*, Coll. Works 5 (Munich 1974) pp. 195-340, esp. 230ff; *Geschichte der Leben-Jesu-Forschung* (Tübingen [6]1951) p. 413f; E. Grässer *Albert Schweitzer als Theologe* (Tübingen 1979) p. 86f. For criticism of this idea see Kümmel *Theologie NT*, p. 43ff.

17. See Merklein 'Die Gottesherrschaft als Handlungsprinzip' 72-107.

18. J. Blank 'Kirche und Staat im Urchristentum' *Kirche und Staat auf Distanz* ed. G. Denzler (Munich 1977) 9-28.

19. F. Mussner 'Der Jakobusbrief' HTK XII/1 (Freiburg-Basel-Vienna 1964) para. 8: 'Der Jakobusbrief und die Ethik Jesu' p. 47ff. According to Mussner: 'There is so much common material in James and Q, that it is hard to dispute that James had knowledge of the Q ethical tradition, as it is collected in the Logia Source.' (p. 51).

20. See Billerbeck *Kommentar zum Neuen Testament aus Talmud und Midrasch* (Munich [2]1956) IV, 1: 'Die altjüdische Privatwohltätigkeit' pp. 536-558; 'Die altjüdische Liebeswerk', pp. 559-610.

21. On this problem see the important work by Ch. Munier *L'Eglise dans l'Empire Romain (II-III siècles)* in the series *Histoire du Droit et des Institutions de l'Eglise en occident*, Bk II, III (Paris 1979).

22. See V. Warnach *Agape. Die Liebe als Grundmotiv der neutestamentlichen Theologie* (Düsseldorf 1951); C. Spicq *Agape dans le Nouveau Testament*, 3 vols. (Paris 1958/9).

23. On Mark 12:28-34, see R. Pesch 'Das Markusevangelium' HTK II/2 (Freiburg-Basel-Vienna 1977) 236-249; J. Gnilka 'Das Evangelium nach Markus' Ekk II/2 (Neukirchen 1979) 162-168.

24. Augustine *In Epistolam Johannis ad Parthos*, Prologus.

F

Richard McCormick

The Teaching Office as a Guarantor of Unity in Morality

THE CHURCH teaches in many ways: through the example of life-style, by sacramental action, through the preached liturgical word, by explicit teaching. Furthermore, such teaching occurs at many levels: Roman, national, diocesan, parochial, familial, individual. Therefore it is clear that all members of the Church, in a variety of roles, are *magistri*, as Bishop B. C. Butler has noted.[1] In this broad sense, all of us pertain to the teaching office of the Church and are responsible guarantors of ecclesiastical unity.

However, the bishops, together with the bishop of Rome, have been entrusted with a very special collegial witness to apostolic tradition. This may be called the 'hierarchical *magisterium*' (in contrast, for example, with the *magisterium* of theologians). In this essay, the teaching office of the Church will be understood in its most narrow sense, as identical with the hierarchical *magisterium*. To explore how such a *magisterium* ought to function as a guarantor of unity in moral (ethical) matters, it would be useful to elaborate two points: (1) the manner of hierarchical teaching; (2) the notion of unity.

1. THE MANNER OF HIERARCHICAL TEACHING

Catholics view the *magisterium* (= hierarchical *magisterium*) as an irreplaceable value. Deprived of it, we would all suffer. However, if we are to continue to enjoy this value, this privilege, the *magisterium* must be rehabilitated, brought abreast of contemporary realities. Teaching in the Church must reflect what contemporary man understands by teaching. This rehabilitation will mean rethinking the meaning of the authentic teaching office. In my judgment, the result of this refashioning will take the direction of a *magisterium* in which we all have a much greater responsibility. That should come as no surprise. If the Christian life is *community* life, life in a collectivity, then Christian moral theology is simply the community trying to discover how best to preserve and express its charity. In summary: the *magisterium* is both a privilege and a responsibility. If we are to continue to enjoy the privilege, we must shoulder the responsibility we have within the magisterial process.

In pursuit of this point, we may offer two scenarios of the *magisterium*.[2] The one will be 'pre-conciliar', the other 'post-conciliar'. By 'pre-conciliar' I mean roughly the period from the Council of Trent to Vatican II. 'Post-conciliar' means after Vatican II. The notion of teaching in the Church has been affected by many cultural variables peculiar to these two periods. Since the Council of Trent, the cumulative effect of these variables has been a notion of teaching, of the *magisterium*, that was highly authoritarian and paternalistic.

(a) Pre-conciliar *Magisterium* and the Cultural Variables that Generated It

Self-definition of the Church. In the pre-conciliar past a rather one-sidedly juridical model of the Church prevailed. The Church was often described along lines closely resembling civil society. Such a description highlighted a vertical or pyramidal structure. In this structure authority as well as truth was seen as descending from the summit down, from the popes and bishops to the priests, and ultimately to the laity. Indeed, the word 'Church' was frequently identified with a small group in positions of authority.

The influence of the mass media. In the pre-jet and pre-television decades access to information and thought in other areas of the world was slow and even restricted, and hence less influential on the formation of opinion. Because opinions were formed with less exposure to other currents of thought, ecclesiastical directives did not always incarnate the full richness of varying traditions and were received less critically within the Church. This means that at times it was possible for them to retain a formative influence disproportionate to their inherent persuasive force.

The awareness of the complexity of issues. In the past Catholic education was not infrequently defensive and cloistered from the major currents of secular life. Similarly many seminaries were isolated from university life. This meant that Catholic attitudes (both theological tenets and language) were formed or maintained apart from the enlightenment that contemporary science could bring to them, and hence without a sufficiently full awareness of the complexity of the issues.

The manner of the exercise of authority in the Church. In the past, authority in the Church was highly centralised both at the Roman and the diocesan level. Where teaching was concerned there was very limited consultation in the drafting of papal statements, and what there was, was often the product of a single theological emphasis. Furthermore, in the decades following the definition of papal infallibility, theologians were a bit overawed by the documents of the ordinary non-infallible *magisterium*. They tended to be almost exegetical in their approach to these teachings and it was close to unthinkable (and certainly very risky) to question the formulation of such documents. These considerations justify the conclusion of Roderick Mackenzie, SJ, that 'between the two Vatican councils there has been a tendency to exaggerate, or to broaden unduly, the role of *magisterium*, and that the Church has suffered on this account'.[3]

Educational status of the clergy and laity. For centuries the clergy were the best educated people in the world. Many cultural factors—among them the broad, non-specialised character of education—explained this phenomenon.

Status of relations between ecclesial groups. In the pre-conciliar era the apologetic or defensive attitude was taken for granted. Our basic attitudes were simply unecumenical. Viewing other ecclesial groups as in some sense 'the adversary', we hardly would turn to these groups for Christian or theological enlightenment. They were not regarded as a reliable source of religious knowledge.

The educational theories and styles dominant in a particular culture. For the past several hundred years, the 'master concept' of education was (and still is in some places) dominant. According to this concept education is basically the handing down of wisdom, experience and research of the professor to a rather passive and non-participative audience of students.

It could be argued that the cumulative effect of influences such as these (more could be adduced) was the formation and settling of a notion of teaching in the Church which manifested three characteristics: (i) it unduly distinguished and separated the *docens* and *discens* function, with a consequent almost unique emphasis on the right to teach, little being said about the duty incumbent on the teacher to learn; (ii) it unduly identified the teaching function in the Church with a single group in the Church (the hierarchy); (iii) it unduly isolated a single aspect of the teaching function (the judgmental). Such a general notion of teaching in the Church narrowed the meaning of the term *magisterium*. It came to be synonymous with the hierarchial issuance of authoritative judgments.

Obviously this notion of teaching influenced both the theology of the *magisterium* and the style of its exercise. First of all, the theology of the *magisterium* so understood laid heavy stress on the authority of the teacher and a correspondingly lesser stress on evidence and the processes whereby it is gathered. In this perspective Christian unity was too easily identified with theological uniformity. Second and correlatively, a theology of response to authoritative teaching developed which was heavily obediential in emphasis. Third, theologians tended to be viewed as agents of the hierarchy whose major, and perhaps even sole, task was to mediate and apply authoritative teaching. Their creative efforts—their more proper educational and theological task—were viewed with distrust. The result of this, of course, was a polarisation between theologians and hierarchy, a growing lack of exchange and communication.

In such circumstances unity could be and was viewed as a reality achieved by authoritative statement. This was clearly the view of Pius XII in *Humani generis*. In that encyclical, the Holy Father stated that once the supreme authority intervened in a disputed question, the matter was no longer a subject of legitimate theological discussion. It has become clear, I believe, that such 'unity' is deceptive. It is not a unity of moral conviction.

(b) Post-conciliar *Magisterium* and Some Cultural Variables that Generated It

The self-definition of the Church. Vatican II provided a new self-definition of the Church as the people of God, a *communio*. In this concentric rather than pyramidal model of the Church, it is the people of God who are the repository of Christian revelation and wisdom. As Leon Cardinal Suenens has pointed out in a recent interview:

> 'The Church, seen from the starting point of baptism rather than that of the hierarchy, thus appeared from the first as a sacramental and mystical reality first and foremost, rather than—which it also is—a juridical society. It rested on its base, the people of God, rather than on its summit, the hierarchy. The pyramid of the old manuals was reversed.'[4]

Obviously such a model suggests, among other things, the need of broad communication if the wisdom resident in the Church is to be gathered, formulated, and reflected to the world.

The influence of the mass media. There is rapid communication of information and thought in a world dominated by television. Furthermore wide circulation of the weekly news magazines and their continuing fascination with religious news has brought technical theology into the marketplace. The scholar is in our time a populariser whether he likes it or not. This means that the Catholic community is better informed theologically than ever.

Awareness of the complexity of issues. In general, Catholics participate more fully than before in the social and intellectual world about them. This means exposure to many modes of thought and to the enrichment consequent upon the convergence of a variety of special competences. Seminaries have drawn increasingly close to the intellectual life of the university. This type of fuller involvement in the secular world has already produced an atmosphere which highlights the depth and complexity of contemporary theological problems, the many competences necessary for their adequate analysis, and the necessarily tentative character of some earlier formulations.

The manner of the exercise of authority in the Church. With its teaching on the nature of the Church and the collegiality of bishops, Vatican II began a process of decentralisation of authority in the Church. Add to this the fact that the post-conciliar Church lives in a secular world whose institutions are increasingly sensitive to the values of participatory democracy and it is easy to agree with the French bishops when they state: 'We have reached a point of no return. From now on the exercise of authority demands dialogue and a certain measure of responsibility for everyone. The authority needed for the life of any society can only be strengthened as a result.'[5]

Educational status of laity and clergy. Educational specialisation and the widespread availability of higher education mean that the clergy is no longer the best educated group in the Church. Many laymen enjoy special expertise, are capable of relating this expertise to doctrinal issues, and can often express themselves articulately in religious and theological matters. Vatican II explicitly recognises this competence when it stated:

> 'Laymen should also know that it is generally the function of their well-formed Christian conscience to see that the divine law is inscribed in the life of the earthly city. . . . Let the laymen not imagine that his pastors are always such experts that to every problem which arises, however complicated, they can readily give him a concrete solution, or even that such is their mission. Rather, enlightened by Christian wisdom and giving close attention to the teaching authority of the Church, let the layman take on his own distinctive role.'[6]

Status of relations between ecclesial groups. We live in an ecumenical age. We experience a new willingness of the Church to seek answers from and in association with other non-Catholic ecclesial groups. As Vatican II noted: 'In fidelity to conscience, Christians are joined with the rest of men in the search for truth and for the genuine solution to the numerous problems which arise in the life of individuals and from social relationships.'[7]

Educational theories and styles dominant in a particular culture. Contemporary education is much more aware of the need to stimulate the student to self-involvement, to creativity, to experiment. The discussion, the seminar, the cross-disciplinary dialogue are the ways of modern education.

The cumulative effect of these influences has been a renewed notion of teaching in the Church. In contrast with the characteristics associated with an earlier notion of teaching, this renewed approach shows these characteristics: (i) it sees the learning process as an essential part of the teaching process; (ii) it regards teaching as a multi-dimensional function only a single aspect of which is the judgmental; (iii) it therefore sees the teaching function as involving the charisms of many persons, not just that of the hierarchy. The term *magisterium* increasingly suggests above all a pluridimensional function in the Church in which all of us have varying responsibilities.

The repercussions of this notion of teaching in the Church are beginning to appear in both the theology of the *magisterium* and the suggested style of its exercise. First of all, without negating the authoritative character of papal or collegial-episcopal pronouncements, contemporary theology devotes more attention to evidence and sound analysis in assessing the ultimate meaning and value of such teachings. In other words, teaching must persuade, not only command. Second, there is a developing theology of response to authoritative non-infallible teaching which emphasises a docile personal assimilation and appropriation of authentic teaching as the appropriate immediate response, rather than an unquestioning assent. Finally, the creative reflection of theologians and the prophetic charisms of all Christians are seen as utterly essential if the hierarchy is to express the faith in our times in a meaningful, contemporary, and persuasive way. Polarisation between theologians and bishops is, from this point of view, simply disastrous.

In such a renewed view of the *magisterium*, unity is not imposed from the top through authoritative statement. Rather it is the spontaneous emergence of a moral conviction through the harmonious functioning of all components of the Church's teaching-learning process. The hierarchical *magisterium* is the vehicle for the emergence of this shared knowledge.

It is only within such a notion of the *magisterium* that the experience and reflection of the faithful (*sensus fidelium*) can play its true role as a *fons theologiae*, and that theology can exercise its creative and critical role. If unity is sought without the contributions of theological research and the experience and reflection of the faithful, it will be an imposed 'unity', a false one. Moreover, the presumption of truth ordinarily enjoyed by official Church teachers (*charisma veritatis*) will be undermined.

It is the constant temptation of those in authority to identify the possession of authority with the possession of moral truth—even without the contributions of those sources *absolutely* necessary for the accurate formulation of moral conviction. Or what is the same, it is a constant temptation to return a pre-conciliar model of the *magisterium*.

This is illustrated by two different understandings of the *sensus fidelium*.

(i) The experience and reflection of the faithful (*sensus fidelium*) ought to be listened to, but it is the ultimate responsibility of authoritative teachers to determine the truth. For instance, if huge segments of the Church believe that the ordination of women is compatible with the gospel and doctrinal development, yet the Congregation for the Doctrine of the Faith (SCDF) determines otherwise, the SCDF is right because authoritative.

(ii) The experience and reflection of the faithful ought to be listened to and it is absolutely essential to a certain and binding proclamation of moral truth. Concretely, if large segments of the community do not see the arguments and conclusions of an authoritative teacher (particularly a ban or condemnation), it is a sign that the matter is not sufficiently clear, or that it has been badly formulated, or is wrong.

Bishops who share the first view see their task as *telling* the people what is right. Bishops of the second view see their task as *discovering* what is right. Bishops of the first view see moral truth exclusively in terms of authoritative formulations of it. Bishops of the second are more aware of doctrinal development and the changing nature of our concrete personhood. Bishops of the first view see the *magisterium* in terms of certainty and clarity. Bishops of the second are more likely to hesitate, question and doubt. Bishops of the first view see dissent, and even openness, as disloyalty. Those of the second see it as the necessary condition for doctrinal development.

Concretisations of these different views may be seen in two recent documents of the SCDF. The 'Declaration on Certain Questions concerning Sexual Ethics' (*Persona humana*) was severely criticised throughout the theological world. Bernard Häring spoke for many when he noted that 'there speaks in the document not *the* pre-conciliar theology, but a very distinct pre-conciliar theology', the type rejected by Vatican II in its rejection of several preliminary drafts for *Gaudium et spes*.[8]

On the other hand there is the SCDF's splendid 'Declaration on Euthanasia'.[9] This was rightly praised throughout the world. It is nuanced, flexible, sensitive to complexity and obviously reveals the type of broad consultation so clearly absent in *Persona humana*.

In summary, then, to be a credible guarantor of unity in morals, even an accurate one, the teaching office must anchor its procedures in a thoroughly open and contemporary notion of the *magisterium*.

2. THE NOTION OF UNITY

Before conclusions can be drawn about the teaching office as a guarantor of unity in morals, we must first establish the level at which unity is considered essential. A basic distinction may aid us in this quest.

(a) The Distinction between Substance and Formulation

John XXIII called attention to the distinction between the substance of a teaching and its formulation. Vatican II adopted this same distinction. Karl Rahner refers to the same thing when he distinguishes a 'truth in itself and in its abiding validity' and its 'particular historical formulation'.[10] By this he means that dogmas are always presented in context and by means of conceptual models which are subject to change. He uses trans-substantiation and original sin as examples. For this latter, those who accept polygenism must rethink what is meant by saying that Adam is the originator and cause of original sin.

Rahner then applies this to ethics. He states:

'Apart from wholly universal moral norms of an abstract kind, and apart from a radical orientation of human life towards God as the outcome of a supernatural and grace-given self-commitment, there are hardly any particular or individual norms of Christian morality which could be proclaimed by the ordinary or extra-ordinary teaching authorities of the Church in such a way that they could be unequivocally and certainly declared to have the force of dogmas.'[11]

This does not mean, Rahner adds, that certain concrete actions cannot be prescribed or proscribed authoritatively. They can, as demanded by the times. But they pertain to man's *concrete nature* at a given point in history. And this concrete nature is subject to change.

The distinction between substance and formulation can be seen in many concrete moral areas. Let premarital sexual intercourse be the example. For centuries the Church has been concerned to preserve the integrity and viability of sexual intimacy and language. This has led her to view it as the language of covenanted friendship, marriage. She has equivalently been saying that sex and eros are fleeting, fickle and frustrative unless they live in and are supported by *philia*, the friendship of two people who take public responsibility for each other in a bold venture of family-making. In formulating this value-judgment, she has, of course, condemned premarital sexual intimacy. Of such conduct she has at one time or other said the following:

(i) it is morally wrong—that is, something is always missing in such conduct;
(ii) it is wrong because it is *contra bonum prolis*, violative of the procreative atmosphere which is inseparably associated with sexual intimacy;
(iii) it is intrinsically evil, that is, *ex objecto* and regardless of circumstances;
(iv) it is seriously wrong in each act;
(v) there is the presumption of serious guilt on the part of those involved.

I would suggest that the Church's substantial teaching is contained in the first statement. The last four variously involve cultural, philosophical and empirical data that are subject to modification and reformulation. Or as Congar puts it: 'The encyclicals of

Leo XIII and Pius XII are theological. They are not purely the expression of apostolic witness according to the needs of the time, but a *doctrine* of the 'cathedrae magistralis' incorporating data from the natural law, human wisdom, and classical theology.'[12]

Moral theologians are more aware than ever of the distinction between substance and formulation—and, I must add, of the difficulty of applying it. There is, therefore, a new willingness to re-examine past formulations. We know that at a given time our formulations—being the product of limited persons, with limited insight, and with imperfect philosophical and linguistic tools—are only more or less adequate to the substance of our convictions. It is the task of theology constantly to question and challenge these formulations in an effort to reduce their inadequacy. This is not an attack on value or on authority, although unfortunately, it is perceived as such by some elements in the Church.

The assertion of Vatican II distinguishing formulation and substance must be properly understood. Otherwise theology could easily be reduced to word shuffling. If there is a distinction between substance and formulation, there is also an extremely close, indeed inseparable, connection. One might say they are related as are body and soul. The connection is so intimate that it is difficult to know just what the substance is amidst variation of formulation. Indeed it is so intimate that improving a formulation may involve, at times, altering a conclusion.

Failure to make this distinction leads to a quest for unity at the wrong level. It also leads to a view of the teaching office as guarantor of unity at the wrong level. Let AIH (artificial insemination by husband) be an example. Pius XII condemned this (*absolute eliminanda*) on three occasions. Yet in the past twenty-five years many theologians have reapproached this question. While acknowledging Pius XII's substantial concern (the biologising or technologising of marriage), they have been unable to defend the *absolute* exclusion of this procedure. If concrete norms of this type are inherently provisional and simply incapable of being dogmas of the Church, it is a mistake to seek or impose community unity at this level.

(b) Loyalty as Grateful but Critical Personal Assimilation of the teaching of the Magisterium

There are important repercussions of this conclusion for the notion of dissent in the Church. John Paul II's book, *The Acting Person*, can serve to illustrate this.[13] The then Cardinal Wojtyla discusses authentic community. There are three characteristics that distinguish authentic community: solidarity, opposition, dialogue. Solidarity 'is the attitude of a community, in which the common good properly conditions and initiates participation'. It refers to a readiness 'to accept and realise one's share in the community'.

Opposition Wojtyla sees as 'essentially an attitude of solidarity'. It is the attitude of those who, because they are deeply devoted to the common good, disagree with official ideas and policies. Of such opposition the Cardinal of Krakow makes several statements: 'The one who voices his opposition to the general or particular rules or regulations of the community does not thereby reject his membership.' Indeed, such opposition is vital to the community's growth and well-being. It is 'essentially constructive'. He continues:

'In order for opposition to be constructive, the structure, and beyond it the ststem of communities of a given society must be such as to allow opposition that emerges from the soil of solidarity not only to *express* itself within the framework of the given community but also to *operate* for its benefit. The structure of a human community is correct only if it admits not just the presence of a justified opposition but also that practical effectiveness of opposition required by the common good and the right of participation.'[14]

Then there is dialogue. Dialogue allows us to 'select and bring to light what in controversial situations is right and true'. Wojtyla admits that dialogue involves strains and difficulties and is sometimes messy. But a 'constructive communal life' cannot exist without it. Opposed to solidarity and opposition are 'inauthentic' attitudes of 'servile conformism' and 'non-involvement'. For example, 'conformism brings uniformity rather than unity'.

Cardinal Wojtyla did not apply this analysis to the ecclesial community. 'But', as Gregory Baum notes, 'the characteristics of authenticity defined for a true community, any true community, secular or religious, ought to apply *a fortiori* to the Church, which is the divine revelation of the model of community in the world.'[15] Baum's point was also made tellingly by both Ronald Modras and Edward Cuddy.[16] For instance, Modras, adverting to *The Acting Person*, correctly asserts that 'loyal opposition can serve the well-being of a Church as well as of a State'. But the situation in Poland did not allow Cardinal Wojtyla to highlight the critical function of theology. The militant hostility of a Marxist régime required a united resistance.

One of the standard responses to this direction of thought is that the people have a 'right not to be confused' ('troubled' is the word used by the Holy Father). The implication frequently made is that theologians should cease expressing their views publicly if those views deviate at all from official formulations. That is, I think, unrealistic and intolerable. As for the 'confusion' of the people, several things need to be said. First, reality is sometimes confusing and it takes time and groping before a truly satisfactory Christian and Catholic response can be formulated. Second, rather than silence free thought and speech in the Church, people must be educated to the idea that differing times do suggest differing perspectives and analyses, especially where very detailed moral norms are concerned, and that what seems a closed question very often is not. Third, they must be educated to the idea that our unity as a community does not ride or fall with absolute uniformity on the application of moral norms to very detailed questions (e.g., *in vitro* fertilisation with embryo transfer). Otherwise the Holy Father's notion of opposition would be only destructive. Finally, they must be educated to take theologians seriously, but not all that seriously. If theologians are mistakenly thought to be the ultimate teachers in the Church, they risk losing, besides their freedom to probe and question, their humility.

These reflections have very important implications for the reformulation of §25 of *Lumen gentium*, particularly of the notion of the 'religious submission of will and of mind' to authentic non-infallible teaching. Recently several theologians have adverted to the need to nuance §25 on the response due to authoritative utterances.[17] I suggest that the proper response is not obedience. Obedience is appropriate when orders are involved. But teaching should not be conceived in this way—and if it is, it shows that we have overjuridicised the search for truth.

Rather, the proper response is first a docility of mind and will, a cast of mind and bent of will open and eager to make the wisdom of the teacher one's own, a desire to surmount the privacy and limitation of one's own views to enjoy the wisdom of broader perspectives. It is, in brief, a desire to assimilate the teaching.

This docility will translate itself into very concrete steps. It will contain and manifest respect for the person and his office, and an openness to his teaching. Secondly, it will imply a readiness to reassess one's own position in light of the teaching. Thirdly, it will involve a reluctance to conclude to certain error. For presumably the teaching was elaborated only after broad consultation and involved the reflections and insights of many in the Church. (However, reluctance is only reluctance.) Finally, appropriate docility will encompass behaviour in the public forum that fosters respect for the teacher. If one does these things, he/she has responded in a manner proportionate to the authority of the teacher. One has indeed brought a response one brings to no other teacher.

This 'docile attempt to assimilate' is the response that was suggested by a statement attributed to the Canadian bishops after the appearance of *Humanae Vitae*. They stated:

> In the presence of other (non-infallible) authoritative teaching, exercised either by the Holy Father or by the collectivity of the bishops he must listen with respect, with openness and with the firm conviction that his personal opinion, or even the opinion of a number of theologians ranks very much below the level of such teaching. His attitude must be one of desire to assent, a respectful acceptance of truth that has upon it the seal of God's Church.[18]

More recently Bishop B. C. Butler has turned his attention to this matter.[19] He points out that the claim of some teachings is, of course, identical with the claim of divine revelation itself. However, he continues, 'to require the same adhesion for doctrines that are indeed taught by officials with authority but to which the Church has not irrevocably committed herself is to abuse authority'. What is the proper response? Butler refers to the 'respect that is due to the considered actions and utterances of those in positions of legitimate and official authority'. More specifically, 'the mood of the devout believer will be . . . a welcoming gratitude that goes along with the keen alertness of a critical mind, and with a good will concerned to play its part both in the purification and the development of the Church's understanding of her inheritance. . . .'

I believe that is a fine statement of the point I am making. When Bishop Butler speaks of 'respect and welcoming gratitude' combined with a 'critical mind' and 'good will concerned to play its part in the purification and development', he has put the matter as well as it can be put. The theologian is in the service of the Church. He serves it well neither by uncritical obedience nor by disrespectul defiance, for neither of these contributes to the 'purification and development of the Church's understanding of her inheritance'. If Butler's 'keen alertness with a critical mind' means anything, it implies the possibility of disagreement, and precisely as part of that 'good will concerned to play its part both in the purification and development . . .'. If such disagreement is experienced as a threat and treated as such, something is wrong.

In other words, the effort to articulate our faith and its behavioural implications in our time is a dialogical and processive one. This point was specifically highlighted by Bernard Häring in a recent essay. He noted:

> There is no doubt that for her own growth, for her abiding in the truth, and for the fruitful exercise of her pastoral *magisterium*, the Church needs an atmosphere of freedom to examine the enduring validity of traditional norms, and the right of a sincere conscience humbly to doubt about norms which, in many or even most of the cases, are not accepted by sincere Christians.

Here Häring and Bishop Butler are at one.[20]

This is how the 'religious submission of will and of mind' (§25, *Dogmatic Constitution on the Church*) ought to be understood. It is not unthinking and uncritical assent.

If this is the appropriate response to authoritative but non-infallible moral teaching, then several things are immediately clear. First, the attempt to assimilate that ends in failure (dissent, or inability to assent) is not only a temporary end to an arduous, prayerful process. It is also a beginning—a beginning of new learning in the Church. To say otherwise is to rule personal reflection out of order in the teaching-learning process of the Church. Concretely, if after the appearance of *Humanae Vitae*, many competent and demonstrably loyal Catholics (bishops, theologians, well educated lay persons) found themselves in a position of modified dissent, this dissent has to be viewed as new evidence. Otherwise we have locked the teaching-learning *process* of the Church into static, juridical structures and moments.

Second, if docile but critical personal assimilation is the proper response to authentic moral formulations of the *magisterium*, it follows that loyalty is not to be located precisely in assent or acceptance of a teaching, but in one's openness and responsibility in attempting to appropriate the teaching. This is extremely important in its practical implications. For there still remain far too many places where questioning and disagreement with 'official' formulations is viewed and treated as disloyalty and disobedience. Quite the contrary is the case. It is the theologian or bishop who fails to state openly and clearly his doubts and misgivings who is disloyal. For he is depriving the *magisterium* of the personal reflection that is utterly essential to its continued good health and well-being.

In summary, then, it can be said that the enormous value of an authoritative *magisterium* will be preserved in our time only if we use it as both privilege and responsibility, sc., as something from which we receive but also as something to which we must contribute. If we are to continue to enjoy the privilege, we must have the courage to incur the responsibility.

Notes

1. B. C. Butler 'Authority and the Christian Conscience' *Clergy Review* 60 (1975) 3-17.
2. I summarise these reflections from my paper 'The Contemporary Moral Magisterium' in *Lectureship* (edited and published privately by Moung Angel Abbey, Oregon).
3. Roderick Mackenzie, SJ 'The Function of Scholars in Forming the Judgment of the Church' in *Theology of Renewal*, ed. L. K. Shook (Montreal 1968) 126-127.
4. *National Catholic Reporter* 28 May 1969, 6.
5. *National Catholic Reporter* 28 May 1969, 6.
6. *Documents of Vatican II* (ed. Walter Abbott) p. 244.
7. *Ibid*. p. 214.
8. B. Häring 'Reflectionen zur Erklärung der Glaubenskongregation über einige Fragen der Sexualethik *Theologisch-praktische Quartalschrift* 124 (1976) 115-126.
9. *Declaration on Euthanasia* (Vatican City 1980).
10. Karl Rahner 'Basic Observations on the Subject of Changeable and Unchangeable Factors in the Church' *Theological Investigations* 14 (1976) 3-23.
11. *Ibid*. 14.
12. Y. Congar 'Brief historique des formes du "magistère" et des ses relations aver les docteurs' *Revue des sciences phil.et theol*. 60 (1976) 112.
13. Karol Wojtyla *The Acting Person* (Boston 1979).
14. *Ibid*. pp. 286-287.
15. Gregory Baum 'Le Pape et la dissidence' *Relations* 39 (1979) 250-251.
16. Ronald Modras 'Solidarity and Opposition in a Pluralistic Church' *Commonweal* 106 (1979) 493-495; Edward Cuddy 'The Rebel Function in the Church' *ibid*. 495-497.
17. See Karl Rahner 'Theologie und Lehramt' *Stimmen der Zeit* 198 (1980) 363-375; André Naud 'Les voix de l'eglise dans les questions morales' *Science et Esprit* 32 (1980) 161-176.
18. I have taken this quote from a release of Documentary Service, the press department of USCC.
19. See note 1.
20. B. Häring 'Norms and Freedom in Contemporary Catholic Thought' *Theological Studies* 37 (1976) 74.

Wilhelm Korff

Nature or Reason as the Criterion for the Universality of Moral Judgments?

THE QUESTION of the universality of moral judgments does not in any way have its origin in the academic need to trace human behaviour back to some ultimate principle. It is rather connected with the fact that human behaviour is not arbitrary but involves a claim to consistency without which the individual's personal identity and social relationships cannot be maintained. In order to be able to live as human beings people must come to terms with each other, must agree on goals, must co-ordinate their expectations of the results of their action. To this extent every group ethos that develops within a system of social relationships is already an initial answer to what from the point of view of our understanding of man is the ever-urgent presence of this question. The further development and growing complexity of the processes of exchange and communication call for correspondingly more comprehensive solutions which guarantee the cohesiveness of people's relationships even in larger social contexts. Today this necessarily leads to the establishment of an ethical system that will apply to the whole of humankind.

1. ON THE HISTORY OF THE PROBLEM

Whatever the restricted conditions under which this question has continually been posed and has been able to develop its own significance, conditions that have subsequently broadened out more and more, and bearing in mind the pragmatic and functional course taken by the development of the idea of universality, what is decisive is that in addition recourse must necessarily be had to criteria which withdraw the ethical claim from everything that is merely pragmatic and link it to something which is given along with man's essential nature as such. Hence the importance that attaches to the concept which was introduced by the Greek sophists of the fifth century BC of a human nature whose effects could not be attributed to other factors and in which this universal moral standard that is given along with man's essential nature was for the first time explicitly distinguished from any positive historical code as far as its general scope was concerned. This pointed the way for every subsequent genuinely scientific discussion of the central ethical question at issue here. This similarly applies to the concept of reason as the real guiding principle of every nature that was introduced in the context of the Socratic and Platonic critique of the sophists' understanding of nature. Since then reason and nature have in fact provided the two standard points of reference to which appeal is made in consideration of ethical questions and which have a key function in the determination of the universality of moral judgments.

Of course, when these two criteria of reason and nature are defined more closely they are shown to be still inseparable from their history. Neither reason nor nature is a simple entity that defines itself. They are subject to their own history of interpretation that arises from the social and cultural context of the time. To this extent each exposition of them represents a version that belongs to a particular historical perceptual horizon and as such cannot be transferred without mediation to contemporary processes of interpretation. But in every case the perceptual value has been maintained of the double definition involved in the differentiation of reason and nature. Whenever one criterion is rigorously played off against the other, the inevitable result is to limit them in a way that threatens to undermine the claim that they are meant to guarantee the universality of moral judgments. The task thus remains of defining this pair of concepts in their essential context of mutual reference in a new and more suitable way as the criteria of the universality of moral judgments, and to do this against the background of the understanding of reason and nature that has developed on the basis of the present state of philosophical inquiry.

2. ANOTHER RETURN TO NATURE

If we start by taking as our standard the general climate of opinion, the first thing to be established is that at present a far-reaching tendency is prominent in the assessment of these two criteria. The balance is tipping towards nature. What has predominated in recent times has been an understanding of reason which, with the emphasis on the responsible individual that it has introduced, has been essentially determined by ideas of autonomy, freedom, emancipation, maturity and progress. But faced with a world that is pushing up against its limits this seems in need of still further exploration in depth. But in this there can certainly be no question—and no doubt should be allowed to remain on this point—of disqualifying as such the basic starting-point for the consideration of reason that we have reached here. If with it totally new approaches have been opened up for mankind of assuring itself of its own potentialities and thereby developing its existence on a more humane basis, this application of human reason does not of course of itself already provide the guarantee of doing justice in every case to the all-embracing context of meaning of this existence and its involvement in the world. To the extent that human reason begins to interpret and shape nature in its own terms, it only too easily runs the risk of forgetting what at the same time this nature is in truth for it itself, namely the foundation on which it is borne.

This is precisely the point at which reason in its relations with reality turns into its opposite and ceases to be a criterion of the universality of moral judgments. This takes place wherever reason ceases to understand itself in its relationship to nature as being at the same time a function of this nature and thus allows nature to degenerate into a mere object, material that can be dealt with as one wishes. The very fact that nature strikes back when its basic requirements are sacrificed, when its ecologies are destroyed and its resources plundered, shows that in the long run there is no viable progress that is not supported by nature. Human reason is the reason of a nature which remains available in its potential that is as powerful as it is fragile only to the extent that man respects the fact that it does not exist solely for his benefit. To this extent what remains fundamentally forbidden to human reason is to make the potential of what man can do without question into the standard of what he ought to do. Man should not do everything he can. Here nature itself sets the unyielding limits.

3. FLIGHT INTO THE IRRATIONAL: THE ABIDING PREROGATIVES OF REASON

But does not this entail the necessity of renouncing reason? Are we not in fact suffering from an excess of reason in view of a development as a result of which future generations run the risk of inheriting only the injuries that have been inflicted on man and the world by what was intended as progress? Are not those prophets of doom and cultural pessimists of the brand of Ivan Illich ultimately right when they warn that contemporary man's interest in the rational penetration and mastery of reality has long become too powerful and that it must therefore finally be shown its limitations? Should we turn our backs on scientific and technological civilisation and return to the simple life? This would be a dangerous false conclusion. Man cannot and may not absolve himself from the responsibilities which have opened up for him and been laid on him in the course of the modern history of reason and freedom. There are no cosy little ecological retreats for five thousand million people.

Against this I venture to put forward the thesis that in fact we are suffering not from an excess but from a deficiency of rationality. One-dimensional technologies of whatever kind ultimately have the effect of destructive factors. The ecological balance of man and the earth as was universally almost taken for granted under the presuppositions of reason before the modern period must today be deliberately and comprehensively encouraged and guaranteed more and more as the condition of future life and indeed of survival in a rationality that is open to learning and correction. There is in fact no longer any sphere of life that man can leave out of his responsibility and relinquish to itself alone. Every growth in knowledge of the reality that surrounds us, every new procedure, every technical invention, every medical advance creates at the same time new ecological, economic, social, physiological and psychological facts, needs, and problems that for their part demand new solutions that will do justice to them. What is involved in all this is of course a rationality that takes into account the whole of life and of the world men and women live in and that understands man's mastery over nature as at the same time the duty of maintaining and developing it.

4. OPTIMISATION AS A CRITERION

What must of course be taken into account in all this is that nature external to man is not an order of pre-established harmony but rather that of a system of equilibrium in flux which, even if it is slowly but continuously changing, tends towards a higher complexity and in whose flux the potentialities thrown up by its creativity are continually being sacrificed to other and newer ones. To this extent conflict is already built in to nature itself, for the sake of its ability to surpass itself and of its continual enhancement. This is intensified in a particular manner when man appears on the scene and, thanks to his reason, begins history. From now on it is human reason that in the forms of human civilisation creates ever new and higher complexities and that on these terms must, on the basis of its own responsibility, a responsibility that ultimately cannot be delegated, adjust itself to the nature that in this way has become its *dominium*, the field over which it exercises mastery, but that nevertheless still sustains it. The conflicts that have to be overcome here gain their particular nature from the fact that, as a being caught up in the mutual involvement of nature and civilisation, man is guided towards creating in the forms of civilisation what is as it were a second, artificial world which as such only becomes possible on the basis of the inroads his reason makes on the world of nature to order and shape it and which because of this reason's essential openness to making projects and learning is liable to much greater and quicker changes than the nature itself which underlies it.

As a result the possibility arises more frequently of functional mismatchings that in certain circumstances can have extremely serious consequences. Although reason, which has truth as its object, is of its nature capable of perceiving what is and what ought to be, nevertheless as a finite created entity it is subject to the possibility of error. This means that in its actual process of discovering the truth there recurs that law of trial and error that in another form is already displayed in the procedure of irrational nature. In what it does it is incapable of surveying everything but for the most part ultimately seizes on the optimal possibility from what emerges as the result of its immediate past activity. It can of course try to swim against this tide by collecting experience and methodically broadening its awareness so that many unnecessary mistakes can be avoided. But the fact that even this does not take place consistently is due to yet another factor that distinguishes reason from nature as such: its liability to temptation, its ability to go against its better judgment and make itself subservient to the impulses and interests that predominantly motivate it at the time. This leads to carelessness, delusion, cynicism, or whatever can develop in the way of irresponsible attitudes which do not allow of any additional indulgence.

Nevertheless the fact remains without a doubt that even when reason is marked by a willingness to learn and an openness to correction it cannot leave nature undamaged in its efforts to create order and pattern. There remains a residue of functional mismatchings as a consequence. This is not only because very often it can only approximate to an accurate determination of the consequences of its intervention that have to be taken into account, but also essentially for the reason that there are no completely disadvantage-proof and conflict-free solutions in the structural relationship between nature and civilisation if one is to attain new patterns of meaning that bring the element of humanity on to a higher level. Everything has its cost; there is no seamless web. There is no such thing as a conflict-free morality for man as a civilised being involved with nature. Expectation and judgment remain his constant companions. All he can consistently attain is what at the moment is the greatest possible degree of reduction of conflict. This, however, occurs when he succeeds in creating relatively stable complexities in which the elements in conflict are adjusted to each other to the best possible degree. But once again it is precisely this that can only be attained by means of the greatest possible investment of reason.

5. REASON AS A PRINCIPLE OF THE INTERPRETATION OF THE ETHICAL

Against this background it should now be completely clear that the moral imperative to bring human reason in its intellectual penetration and civilising shaping of the reality of the world to its complete maturity cannot in any way be identified with a naive belief in reason and progress. What in fact indicates the maturity of reason is that of its own nature it has to show itself as reason in nature, as something which remains constitutionally determined by the experience of the finiteness of its potentialities. It is precisely this that in truth prevents it from linking with the idea of progress the idea of totality, of the achievability of ultimate human happiness. All that can be attained in the conditions of this world is a relative happiness and success of material things, not, however, the perfection of the entire totality. For this reason it is as foolish as it is dangerous to introduce prematurely a credulous belief in reason in order to play it off against a new credulous belief in nature.

What in fact would be obtained by such a counter-proposal of making nature in its opposition to reason the immediate standard for moral judgments? To reduce it to the lowest common denominator, reason would be whittled down to a mere organ for reading off what had been determined elsewhere. Everything that comprises the ethical component of human activity would have to be provided by nature, and in this context especially by human nature as such. This, however, is not the case. What according to its nature this nature could be as an ethical criterion is not self-evident. The reason is that by nature man is genuinely ordered as a being of civilisation, with the result that every appeal to his nature as the standard for moral judgments is an appeal to a nature that is already interpreted by rational activity and to this extent interpreted in a manner specific to civilisation. This applies even in those cases when, in contrast to a pattern of civilisation that has become extremely artificial, the attempt is made to ascertain what is and has its effects on the basis of nature alone in order to develop standards of behaviour that are as close to nature as possible. Even these cannot be discovered and established without rational exertion, nor maintained without methodical—which once again means completely artificial—efforts at classification. This applies to reliance for energy on 'natural' sources that are capable of regeneration just as much as to 'natural' forms of nutrition, 'natural' forms of medical treatment or 'natural' methods of birth control. But without regard for this such 'natural' models of behaviour have their own moral appeal in the face of a world that has become extremely artificial with the dynamic quality that pertains to it. To the extent that man exposes to doubt the products of his reason with their tendency to autonomy and refuses them blind obedience, they acquire a corrective function that should not be underestimated. But on the other hand the question remains whether nature in this is not as a whole interpreted in too restrictive a sense if it is only these 'natural' examples of behaviour that are to be regarded as in keeping with the meaning that is inherent in nature and is suitable for interpretation and development by reason. The question is intensified if one goes on to set them up as an ethical absolute as the only authentic types of solution. This would in fact mean them losing any plausibility. People would see themselves limited in their opportunities of life and development to conditions far below the measure of what is rationally possible, necessary and responsible. The 'naturalness' of rules of behaviour is thus clearly not also a guarantee of their universal applicability.

6.   THE SETTING OF LIMITS AS NATURE'S FUNCTION

If therefore nature as opposed to reason should turn out to be the criterion for the universal validity of moral judgments, then one ought not to look for this universal validity in something it does not provide on its own account, in other words in ethical norms that are supposedly built into it and 'discoverable' in it *a priori*. Ethical norms are not properties of nature but the results of interpretation by reason. As the organ that brings everything that is into awareness, evaluates it and develops it to the relevant possible limit, this latter alone is the principle for the interpretation and fulfilment of moral behaviour. Nature does however have a contribution of its own to make to the establishment of the universal validity of the pattern of moral judgments disclosed thanks to reason. This is something that arises from the structure and composition of this reason itself. It is reason situated in nature and thus in an immensely complicated relational context of laws that share in conditioning each of its steps, whether by making them possible and encouraging them or by limiting and restricting them.

This is precisely the point that Thomas Aquinas was aiming at in the context of his doctrine of natural law, with on the one hand the concept of *inclinationes naturales* as the inward sphere of motivation of specific natural tendencies that fundamentally is responsible for human behaviour, and on the other with the concept of *determinatio* as the factual constraints of its structural environment that shape and limit this behaviour.[1] But this means that according to St Thomas all human behaviour remains universally determined by conditions which may not replace reason, since they need interpretation and to this extent do not present themselves as ethical norms, but which nevertheless eliminate arbitrariness from this behaviour in all its realisations. For the formation of a critically based moral judgment it can of course no longer be enough today to assure oneself of factors at work and conditioning laws of this kind that come into play and have to be taken into account, as happens with St Thomas, over and above mere ordinary reason in the form of simple empirical procedures. The contexts have in fact turned out to be very much more complex and many-layered. To investigate them and thus to prepare the way for the formation of an adequate ethical judgment is today the task of a multiplicity of individual disciplines in the human and social sciences.[2] This is particularly clear in the field of material ethical questions. The more ethics becomes concrete as opposed to abstract ethics, the more weight for the process of discovering norms with reference to whatever fields of action are under consideration attaches to the laws disclosed by these various individual disciplines, laws which ethics is not able to construct on its own account. But analysis also reveals to an ever greater extent fundamental contexts which sustain and determine human behaviour and are of general importance for moral behaviour form the point of view of man's structural development. This applies especially with reference to the perception of those fundamental inter-acting conditioning laws which provide the general structure both for human association and for the search for human identity and thus protect both from arbitrary intervention.[3]

7. THE CONSTITUTION OF MAN AS A MORAL SUBJECT

Whatever recognisable or even hidden pre-existing elements of nature may be at the disposal of the rational processes of decision with regard to moral behaviour, the principle of moral action nevertheless remains not nature but reason. It is reason alone that puts man in a position to distinguish between good and evil. This ability belongs to reason of its nature and is specific to it in just as elementary a fashion as the ability to distinguish between true and false. In the one case its point of reference is the determination of what is or is not, in the other of what ought or ought not to be. It is one of St Thomas's valid discoveries to have shown that in one case as in the other reason, whether as theoretical or practical reason, is in all its acts subject to one and the same basic law of logic: it is designed not to act against itself in contradiction. The first and most general principle of the practical reason considered in relation to behaviour, namely that good is to be done and striven for and evil avoided, ultimately follows the same law of contradiction from which the difference between true and false is derived for the theoretical reason.[4] Man cannot describe as simultaneously true and false one and the same state of affairs with reference to one and the same set of basic circumstances. Nor can he describe a particular action with reference to one and the same set of basic circumstances as morally good and at the same time as morally bad, as evil. Thus in the field of action, too, reason wants to experience agreement with itself, with the basic circumstances evident to it. From this we gain, even before any further determination of the content of good and evil, a formal concept of guilt that derives from the subjective rational act of the individual: guilt is behaviour against one's own better judgment and conviction.

But even the fundamental standard of moral behaviour that is the supreme standard provided by the dignity of the human person gains its power of conviction not from what is also provided by nature but from the constitution of man as a moral subject by reason. It is only to the extent that man makes the inviolability of being a human person, directed as it is to reason and freedom, into the general guiding principle of his behaviour and thus prevents any dealings with himself and with others from being at the disposal of arbitrary whims—it is only to this extent that a criterion is obtained that guarantees the universal validity of moral judgments with regard to their highest and at the same time most elementary area of concern. To have shown this is the achievement of Kant. But the normative consequence that it also contains for man's dealings with nature must also be deduced from this same criterion. For if it is reason that qualifies being a human person and endows it with dignity, and if for its part this same reason recognises the foundation that sustains it in pre-existing nature, then man cannot abandon his responsibility for nature without at the same time sacrificing his dignity as a rational being. Personal dignity includes of its very essence a supreme value with regard to responsible relations with nature.

Nevertheless the question remains whether the ultimate element of human dignity has in fact been comprehended and secured with this fundamental act of man's self-obligation to his dignity as a rational being. What is the source of the absolute quality of this will to reason, to dignity, to truth? What gives man the reason for accepting himself and others in circumstances when there is no hint of reason, when injustice, misery and powerlessness, guilt and wickedness replace the traces of this reason until it cannot be discerned? How can this remain thinkable if the universal claim of human dignity and thereby the universal validity of moral judgments are not comprehended on the basis of a reason that transcends all finite, created reason: the reason of God himself that reveals itself as grace and guarantees the definitive sense and meaning of human existence? But this is something that is only disclosed by faith.

Translated by Robert Nowell

Notes

1. See Thomas Aquinas *Summa Theologiae* 1a. 2ae. Q.94, 2 and 95, 2.
2. See W. Korff 'Wege empirischer Argumentation' in *Handbuch der christlichen Ethik* I, ed. A. Hertz, W. Korff, T. Rendtorff and H. Ringeling (Freiburg-im-Breisgau/Basle/Vienna 1978) pp. 83-107.
3. See W. Korff *Norm und Sittlichkeit. Untersuchungen zur Logik der normativen Vernunft* (Mainz 1973) pp. 76-112; W. Korff 'Die naturale und geschichtliche Unbeliebigkeit menschlicher Normativität' in *Handbuch der christlichen Ethik* I pp. 147-164; and G. W. Hunold 'Identitätstheorie: Die sittliche Struktur des Individuellen im Sozialen' *ibid*. pp. 177-195.
4. See St Thomas Aquinas *Summa Theologiae* 1a. 2ae. 94, 2 and 95, 2.

Joseph Komonchak

Moral Pluralism and the Unity of the Church

THE ISSUE arises because the Church is confessed to be one and catholic not only in its apostolic faith but also in its holiness—*una sancta catholica*. It is by an 'orthopraxis' of love, Jesus said, that his disciples would be recognisable (John 13:35) and the Father's love for men be known (John 17:23-26). The things Jesus said are not only truths to be known, but a truth to be *done* (John 13:17). Not everyone who says, 'Lord, Lord', will enter the Kingdom, but he who does the will of the Father (Matt. 7:21; and see vv. 28:20).

Such communal holiness is always a very concrete matter, not merely words and speech but deed and truth (1 John 3:18). It is not realised only by a community of moral *teaching*, but must show itself in a transformed communal existence. The unity which derives from the grace and gifts of the one God (*unitas de Trinitate*) becomes actual and effective only as an accomplishment of each successive generation of Christians (*unitas ex hominibus*).

But the very concreteness of the realisation of a holy communion raises the problem this issue of *Concilium* addresses. For the holy communion is not only to be one but also catholic, and it can only be catholic if it is concrete, accomplished or realised here, there, and everywhere, yesterday, today and tomorrow. What may unify the Church in one place or at one time may not be what unifies the Church in another place or at another time. And yet the catholic diversity cannot destroy the unity of the Church universal.

The question of the moral or practical unity of the Church thus revolves around two poles, the concrete moral demands of particular situations and the common and universal principles of Christian living. The question is what degree of diversity in judgments about the concrete *bonum faciendum* is compatible with moral communion. The following pages attempt some methodological clarifications and distinctions which might permit a nuanced assessment. They are both anthropological and ecclesiological. I will distinguish: (1) the generative principles of Christian morality; (2) the mediating principles of Christian moral inquiry; and (3) the concrete context of Christian moral unity-in-action.

1. THE GENERATIVE PRINCIPLES OF CHRISTIAN MORALITY

By generative principles I mean something like the first and universal principles which ground and distinguish Christian moral activity. Rather than call them first principles, however, which may suggest the premises of a deductive logic, I call them 'generative' principles to indicate that they provide the existential and productive basis for both the process and the criteria of moral discernment.

There are two such principles, one objective and the other subjective. There are, first, objective reference-points to which Christians commonly refer in making theoretical or practical moral judgments. Among them are the Scriptures, the Church's moral tradition, the example of holy lives, past and present, the common sacramental life, and a concrete community of Christian moral sensibility. While there are disagreements about the relative weight to be assigned to each of these carriers of Christian moral authority, such reference-points must exist and function or the question of moral unity among Christians cannot even arise.

The second generative principle is subjective, the converted selves of Christians. The new law of Christ is the grace of the one Holy Spirit poured out upon all God's children and effecting a transvaluation of the personal centre and source of values. Whatever the metaphors used to describe it, at the heart of Christian existence is an experience of transformation whose immediate effect is a newly oriented self, committed now to what it had not loved before, discovering a new world to live in and to make come to be. The subjective principle of Christian moral activity is the Christian himself as an 'originating value',[1] the existential subject of a moral sensitivity become 'connatural'.

There is an existential priority of the subjective principle to the objective, for only by such conversion is the merely potential authority of the objective reference-points made actual and effective. On the other hand, there is an interpretative or hermeneutical priority of the objective principle to the subjective, for of itself the subjective experience may be conscious, but it will not be properly understood or known without the objective reference-points. Similarly, the unity of the Church in its moral practice is only potential by virtue of a common acceptance of the objective authority; moral communion among the members of the Church is effectively realised only when a common experience of conversion brings them together in a common love of God and neighbour, interpreted and directed by the objective representations of Christian meaning and value.

2. THE MEDIATION OF CHRISTIAN MORAL INQUIRY

Christian moral community is not realised in the abstract but only in a concrete community of values, goals and means responding to the moral demands of particular situations. Between the common generative principles and concrete situations and experiences of Christian responsibility, there must intervene a mediating process of interpretation, discovery, and application. For no objective principles can envisage all possible situations, and love (or whatever other term is used for the subjective principle) does not substitute for knowledge.

The mediating principles of Christian moral inquiry will include the following elements:

(a) A foundational anthropology, universal because foundational. The need for such an anthropology is implied in the universal relevance of the Christian message. It will articulate the main lines of the vision of the human person in the world which arises out of the generative principles, both objective and subjective.

(b) General anthropologies, which develop the moral implications of the 'anthropological constants' implied both in the foundational anthropology and in the unity of the human race.[2] These anthropologies are said to be 'general' both because they are not specific to Christianity and because they are derived from constants that can be derived dialectically from the very existence of cultural pluralism.[3]

(c) Culturally and historically specific anthropologies, which develop the moral implications of the different realisations of the anthropological constants in different times, places and cultures.

(d) Heuristic methods for aiding the concrete discernment, by individuals and communities, of the values required by the foundational, general and specific anthropologies.

These four elements differ greatly in their degree of universalisability. Foundational anthropologies aspire to be universal precisely because they attempt to define the basic situation of every person before God and other persons and in the world. General anthropologies will be general to the degree that morally significant anthropological constants can be discovered in their many realisations in time, place, and culture. Specific anthropologies will not be universalisable to the degree that the cultural and historical realisations of the constants introduce moral dimensions not implied in other realisations. The heuristic methods of moral discernment will vary in universalisability to the degree that they articulate the exigencies of the foundational and general anthropologies or assume, critically or not, the specific anthropologies.

With regard to the moral unity of the Church, the foundational and general anthropologies at least aspire to articulate universal moral exigencies implied in the universal mission of the Church and in the unity of the human race. As legitimate and necessary as this task is, it is not an easy one; it has taken many forms; and, even when successful, must remain at an abstract level. Differences with regard to the specific anthropologies will be compatible with the unity of the Church to the extent that Christianity is not believed in some or all areas to require particular realisations of the anthropological constants. This is commonly admitted for certain areas (economies, polities, for example) but not for others (family, sexuality, for example). Differences in heuristic method will be judged compatible with Church-unity in so far as they draw upon the founding, the general, or the specific anthropologies. Even where these elements conspire to promote a moral communion in the Church, of course, there always remains the diversity that arises out of the irreducible uniqueness of God's call to individual persons precisely as individuals.

If these remarks succeed in introducing some formal clarity, their usefulness is affected by two major methodological difficulties which help to explain much of the disagreement that exists with regard to moral pluralism in the Church.

The first concerns the effort to distinguish between general and specific anthropologies, that is, between anthropological constants and their realisations in different times, places and cultures. That such a distinction can and must be made is not a new discovery; it is in fact found, at least nascently, in Aristotle and Aquinas. But even when specific cultural and historical realisations are not simply identified with the anthropological constants, they may be interpreted ethnocentrically (as when 'civilisaton' is contrasted with 'barbarism') or classicistically (as when the normative or natural is opposed to the aberrant or unnatural); this can amount to a practical denial of the distinction.

As important as it is to invoke theological and philosophical criteria in discriminating between the constants and specific realisations, there is also an indispensable role for the human sciences to play, particularly since in their modern form they take precisely the empirical variety of cultural and historical realisations of the human as the object of their study. The critical introduction of these sciences into the theological task is, however, still very difficult because of the fundamental methodological controversies that bedevil both theology and the human sciences.[4] Many of the differences between opposed interpretations of Christian morality arise here in so far as (a) theologians or churchmen persist in the belief that theology is the 'full science of man',[5] (b) they are willing or unwilling to concede that historical consciousness and the human sciences require them to be much more critical, careful, and modest than they have been in stating what are anthropological constants, or (c) they make use, critical or not, of one or another variety or school of human science to construct the specific anthropologies which mediate the foundational and general anthropologies.

The second methodological problem is that neither the foundational nor the general anthropologies are found in pure form in the generative principles of Christian morality. In the Scriptures, in the tradition, in the example of holy lives, the foundational and the general is already mediated, very often at least, by the culturally and historically specific and by the particular. Holy lives, including that of Christ, are particular realisations of meaning and value within specific contexts and in response to particular situations. They may have (and in the case of Christ do have) universal normative significance, but what is universal in them will not be determined without some such distinctions as those offered above.

Similarly, the Scriptures include not only the example of holy lives, but commandments, counsels, exhortations, etc., as well as various more or less reflective justifications of them. Some of these might even be considered to be early attempts at foundational or general or specific anthropologies, although, of course, these distinctions are seldom present consciously or critically. Of these anthropologies, the foundational may be considered to have greater and even universal normative value; the general will be normative if discernible in the specific; whether the specific should retain any normative value which is the greater question, of course, can only be settled by establishing that it is a necessary implication of either the foundational or the general anthropology. Traditional moral theology has admitted that not all the specific anthropological statements of the Scriptures have enduring normative value; the question today is to found whatever distinctions are made critically and in the light of historical consciousness and the modern human sciences.

These considerations hold *a fortiori* for the Church's moral tradition, which is not merely nor perhaps even principally a matter of teaching and theory but also of practice.

Many of the disagreements with regard to moral pluralism in the Church are related to the two methodological problems briefly described here. They will not be easy to resolve. Until they are resolved, it will surely be of some comfort to remember with Yves Congar that 'unity without oppositions is eschatological';[6] but it remains that certain attitudes towards pluralism not only cause great pain and confusion in individuals but greatly compromise the ability of the Church to offer a common witness and service to the world. Some attention to ecclesiological questions is therefore necessary.

3. THE CONCRETE CONTEXT OF CHRISTIAN MORAL ACTION

A concrete moral decision is the principled response of a Christian to the demands of particular situations. The anthropologies outlined above provide the foundational, general, and specific frameworks within which a Christian seeks to reverse evil and to promote the good. He may find himself in a moral community with others who accept those anthropologies, but the concrete good to be done will always also be a personal contribution which can vary as greatly as do the variety of new selves whom God's love brings forth in the Church. The anthropologies do not serve only as restrictive frameworks, but as the evocative matrices within which quite unique responsibilities can be discerned, embraced, and realised.[7]

On the other hand, it can be asked whether the individual may not also legitimately disagree with the moral positions of the Church. On one level, the distinctions made above may offer some guidelines. It is clear that disavowal, theoretical or practical, of the generative principles is in effect the refusal of Christian moral communion. While this certainly can happen, it is, one hopes, more common for the disagreement to concern the mediation of Christian moral inquiry. Here perhaps we may say that the legitimacy of disagreement may increase as one moves from the foundational and the general to the specific anthropologies and, even more, from the specific anthropology to concrete and particular moral situations.

Without denying this, however, one may note that there are other considerations which are not always taken into account. The discussion of the legitimacy of dissent, not least of all because of the issues around which the debate commonly revolves, often suffers from a certain abstractness. It counterposes an individual and the universal Church (especially when this is considered merely institutionally) or the universal *magisterium*. Both terms of this opposition often neglect the concrete ecclesial context; which is that of the particular or local Church. The issue becomes adequately concrete only when it includes (*a*) the Christian moral responsibility of each particular and local Church in its own situation; (*b*) the relationship between the moral options of individual Churches or between an individual Church and Rome; and (*c*) the relationship between an individual Christian and his particular or local Church.

If the one and universal Church only comes to be in and out of the self-realisations of the particular Churches (Vatican II), then there is a sense also in which the moral unity of the universal Church is constructed 'from below'. Particular Churches are not carbon copies or the identical impressions of a single stamp. They are the communal responses to the Word and grace of God as this is brought to bear upon particular contexts and situations. The Word is not preached in general, but as a Word for *this* context and situation; God's grace does not heal in general, it heals *this* realm of sin; and the new moral communion is an overcoming of the alienations that divide *this* group of people. That is why there must be some ecclesial equivalent of the 'formal existential ethic' which Karl Rahner proposed for the Christian individual.

Now it can happen that what morally unites one particular Church as its realisation of redemptive community will not be what unites another particular Church, and no Church can excuse itself from self-responsibility merely by imitating the self-realisation of another Church. On the other hand, because all the Churches arise out of the same generative principles, the particular Churches can and should not only support one another but also challenge and even criticise one another. The specific anthropologies which mediate the moral discernment of the particular Churches distinguish them within a moral community articulable in the foundational and general anthropologies. And particularly in a world growing increasingly interdependent, even the specific anthropologies and moral options of one Church must pose questions about the responsibilities of other Churches.

The universal Church is mediated to the individual Christian by his particular Church. The immediate reference-point of his moral inquiry is the particular or local self-realisation of Christian community, especially that Eucharistic community which is supposed to provide the community of moral sensibility that is the matrix of his own Christian conscience. It is primarily in and through such communities that the Church is the agent of Christ's redemptive work in the world, and they fulfil this task by addressing the moral issues which face them as concrete and local communities. The individual lives out his Christian life in this communal context, and this community should be the immediate matrix, guide, support, challenge and critic of his moral efforts. Within that community, there should be enough room for his own creative realisation of Christian existence, and, itself never perfect, the local community should not be erected into an infallible authority. But Christian life should not normally be a solitary witness, and among the chief reference-points which an individual must take into account must be the common values and decisions of the fellow-members of his own community. To the degree that members of local communities do not see community of value and action as part of their responsibility, whatever unity the Church may have will be pre-moral and invite the criticism of being simply mythical. It is true, of course, that the more concrete an issue is, the less certainty anyone, including Church leaders, can have about it; but it is also true that a unity which never becomes concrete and effective in common action falls far short of what is required of a Church that claims to be a 'sign and instrument' not only of union with God but also of unity among men (*Lumen Gentium* §1).

CONCLUSION

From all this it is perhaps clear at least that it will be very difficult to lay down hard-and-fast rules for a statement of legitimate moral pluralism in the one Church. This discussion has suggested that it is not adequate to address the issue solely in terms of a vague unity of the Spirit or of unity in some pre-moral, pre-practical moment: the Church's unity must also be a unity-in-praxis. On the other hand, this is not concretely addressed or realised from a universal standpoint. The immediate place for the realisation of the Church's redemptive unity is the local or particular Church, which is also the place where the tensions between cultures and between creative individual and moral community are experienced most acutely and most concretely. Discussions that never reach this level of the Church's self-realisation are guaranteed to be inadequate and ineffective.

Notes

1. The term 'originating value' is taken from Bernard Lonergan's analysis of 'the structure of the human good' in *Method in Theology* (New York 1972) pp. 47-52.
2. The term 'anthropological constants' is employed by Peter Berger and Thomas Luckmann in *The Social Construction of Reality: A Treatise in the Sociology of Knowledge* (Garden City, New York 1967) p. 49. Edward Schillebeeckx attempts a presentation of seven such constants in his book, *Christ: The Experience of Jesus as Lord* (New York) pp. 731-743 (*Gerechtigheid en liefde: Genade en bevrijding*, Bloemendaal 1977).
3. See Wilhelm Dupré 'Ethnocentrism and the Challenge of Cultural Relativity' in *True and False Universality of Christianity*, ed. C. Geffré and J. -P. Jossua (*Concilium* 135; Edinburgh, New York 1980) 3-13.
4. It is the great merit of Bernard Lonergan's work that he has always insisted on the critical reciprocal relationship between method in theology and the methods of the natural and human sciences; see most recently 'The Ongoing Genesis of Methods' *Studies in Religion* 6 (1976/77) 341-355.
5. For the Church to become 'a fully conscious process of self-constitution', Lonergan argues, 'it will have to recognise that theology is not the full science of man, that theology illuminates only certain aspects of human reality', that theology must therefore unite itself 'with all other relevant branches of human studies' (*Method in Theology* p. 364).
6. Yves Congar 'Reflexions et recherches actuelles sur l'assemblee liturgique' *La Maison-Dieu* 115 (1973) 24.
7. Karl Rahner's well known theses on 'formal existential ethics' and on the charismatic dimension in the Church are relevant here, although, as will be argued below, they need to be more closely related to the particular and local ecclesial contexts in which individual Christians experience their unique calls.

Contributors

GEORGETTE ODI ASSAMOI was born in 1943 in Adzope, Ivory Coast. She holds a doctorate from the University of Montpellier, France, and lectures in the Humanities Faculty of the University of Abidjan. She is a catechist and is married with six children.

JOSEF BLANK was born in 1926 in Ludwigshafen on the Rhine and was ordained priest in 1951. He studied at the Universities of Tübingen, Munich, Würzburg. From 1969 he has been professor of New Testament exegesis and Biblical theology at the University of Saarland at Saarbrücken. Among his publications are: *Krisis* (1964), *Paulus und Jesus* (1968), *Schriftsauslegung in Theorie und Praxis* (1969), *Das Evangelium als Garantie der Freiheit* (1970), *Weiss Jesus mehr vom Menschen?* (1971), *Der Mensch am Ende der Moral* (1971), *Jesus von Nazareth. Geschichte und Relevanz* (1972), *Verändert Interpretation den Glauben* (1972), *Das Evangelium nach Johannes. Geistliche Schriftlesung* 4/2 and 3 (1977), *Das Evangelium nach Johannes. Geistliche Schriftlich* 1a and 1b (1981), *Christliche Orientierung* (1981).

CLODOVIS BOFF was born in Brazil in 1944 and is a priest of the Order of the Servants of Mary. He holds a doctorate in theology from the Universtiy of Louvain, and teaches at the Pontifical University of Rio de Janeiro. Besides contributing to several reviews, he is the author of four books, including *Teologia e Prática* (1978), which has been translated into German, Italian and Spanish, and, with Leonardo Boff, *Da Libertacão* (1979).

JULIA CHING is professor of East Asian and Comparative Religions at the University of Toronto (Victoria College). She is China-born, received her doctorate from the Australian National University, and has also taught at Columbia and Yale Universities. Her publications include *Confucianism and Christianity* (1977). Articles by her have appeared several times in *Concilium*.

ENRIQUE DUSSEL was born in Mendoza (Argentine) in 1934. He holds a theology degree and doctorates in philosophy and history, and lectures on ethics and church history in Mexico. He is president of the study commission on the History of the Church in Latin America, and a founder member of the Ecumenical Association of Third World Theologians. He is the author of numerous books dealing with various aspects of the theme of liberation, of which the following have been published in English translations: *Ethics and the Theology of Liberation* (1978), *History of the Church in Latin America, 1492-1980* (1981), *Papers for Liberation Theology* (1981).

WILHELM ERNST was born at Bonenburg in Westphalia in 1927. He was ordained to the priesthood in 1955. He is professor of moral theology and ethics at Erfurt, East Germany. He is a member of the International Theological Commission. He is one of the editors of the *Erfurter Theologische Studien*, the *Erfurter Theologische Schriften*, and the *Theologisches Jahrbuch*. His publications include: *Die Tugendlehre des Franz Suarez* (1964), *Gott und Mensch am Vorabend der Reformation* (1972), and *Ehe im Gespräch* (1978).

ERIC FUCHS was born in Geneva, Switzerland. He was the director of the Centre Protestant d'Etudes (Geneva) from 1960-1979 and joint founder and director of the Atelier oecuménique de théologie (Geneva) from 1973-1980. He is a doctor of theology and lectures in ethics in the Faculties of Theology of Geneva and Lausanne. He is editor of the collection 'Le champ éthique' (Labor et Fides, Geneva). His published works include books on Christian ethics and sexuality and commentaries on II Peter and Jude.

JOSEPH KOMONCHAK was born in Nyack (New York) in 1939 and ordained in 1963. He studied philosophy at St Joseph's Seminary, Yonkers, NY, and theology at the Gregorian University in Rome, from which he received the licentiate in sacred theology in 1964. After serving in a parish for three years, he taught systematic theology at St Joseph's Seminary for ten years. In 1976 he received the doctorate in philosophy from Union Theological Seminary in New York, with a dissertation on the ecclesiology of the young Newman. Since 1977 he has been an associate professor in the Department of Religion and Religious Education at the Catholic University of America, Washington, DC. He has published articles on ecclesiology, *magisterium* and ministry in such journals as *Theological Studies*, *The Thomist*, and *Concilium*.

WILHELM KORFF, born at Hilden in 1926, studied philosophy and theology at Bonn University. In 1973 he was appointed professor of moral theology at Tübingen, and in 1979 moved to Munich as professor of Christian social ethics. His publications include: *Ehre, Prestige, Gewissen* (1966), *Norm und Sittlichkeit. Untersuchungen zur Logik der normativen Vernunft* (1973), *Theologische Ethik. Eine Einführung* (1975), and *Kernenergie und Moraltheologie. Der Beitrag der theologischen Ethik zur Frage allgemeiner Kriterien ethischer Entscheidungsprozesse* (1979). Besides writing numerous articles on questions of social ethics Wilhelm Korff is also one of the editors of the first venture in Catholic-Protestant co-operation in the field of ethics, the *Handbuch der christlichen Ethik* (1978).

RICHARD McCORMICK, SJ, is the Rose F. Kennedy Professor of Christian Ethics, Kennedy Institute of Ethics, Georgetown University. His recent books include: *Doing Evil to Achieve Good* (1978, edited with Paul Ramsey), *How Brave a New World? Dilemmas in Bioethics* (1981), and *Notes on Moral Theology: 1965-1980* (1981).

FRANCIS MURPHY was born in New York City in 1914. He gained an MA (1942) and a PhD (1944) in medieval history from the Catholic University of America, Washington, DC. He was military chaplain from 1944-1947, then parish priest in New York from 1950-1951 and from 1958-1959. He served as professor of patristic moral theology, Academia Alfonsiana, Lateran University, Rome, between 1959-1975. He has been rector of the Holy Redeemer College, Washington, DC, from 1977 to present. A peritus at Vatican Council II (1962-1965), Father Murphy served as staff editor for early Christianity and Byzantine Church History on the *New Catholic Encyclopedia* (1962-1967). He has been visiting professor of humanities and politics, Princeton University (1971-1972), Fellow of the Woodrow Wilson Center for Scholars, Smithsonian Institution (1972-1973); adjunct professor, Politics Department, The John Hopkins University (1973-1975), lecturer at the Folger Shakespeare Library (1976) and participant in international symposia as diverse as the Oxford Patristic Congresses (from 1959 to 1979), UN Population Year, 1974 to the Petrarch Centenary, Thomas More Symposium and the Seminar on Monasticism and the Arts. His publications include: *Rufinus of Aquileia (345-410) His Life and Works* (1945), *A Monument to St Jerome* (1952), *Peter Speaks Through Leo: The Council of Chalcedon, AD 451* (1952),

Politics and the Early Christian (1967), *John Paul II: The Pilgrim Pope* (1979), *Constantinople II, 553 (Histoire des Conciles Oecumeniques 3* (1974), *This Church, These Times* (1980), *The Papacy Today* (1981).

BERNARD QUELQUEJEU, OP, was born in Paris in 1932. After scientific studies which brought him in 1953 to the Ecole Polytechnique, he joined the Dominican Order in 1957. After a licentiate in theology, he obtained a doctorate in philosophy in 1968 from the University of Paris-Nanterre. At present he is professor of anthropology and philosophical ethics at the Institut Catholique in Paris and editor of the *Revue des Sciences philosophiques et théologiques*. His thesis was published under the title *La Volonté dans la philosophie de Hegel* and he has published numerous articles on moral and political philosophy, notably a series of three under the general title 'Karl Marx a-t-il constitué une théorie du pouvoir d'Etat?' in *Rev. Sc. ph. th.* for 1979.

CONCILIUM

All back issues are still in print and available for sale. Orders should be sent to the publishers,

T. & T. CLARK LIMITED

36 George Street, Edinburgh EH2 2LQ, Scotland

X

CONCILIUM
Religion in the Eighties

A multi-volume library of contemporary religious thought • published
in 10 volumes annually • exploring the
latest trends and developments in the Sociology of
Religion, Liturgy, Dogma, Practical Theology,
Fundamental Theology, Canon Law, Ecumenism,
Spirituality and Moral Theology

Edited by

GIUSEPPE ALBERIGO • JOSE LUIS ARANGUREN
GREGORY BAUM • LEONARDO BOFF
ANTOINE VAN DEN BOOGAARD • PAUL BRAND
LUCIANO CAGLIOTI • MARIE-DOMINIQUE CHENU O.P.
JOHN COLEMAN S.J. • MARY COLLINS O.S.B.
YVES CONGAR O.P. • MARIASUSAI DHAVAMONY S.J.
CHRISTIAN DUQUOC O.P. • AUGUST WILHELM VON EIFF
VIRGIL ELIZONDO • ELISABETH SCHÜSSLER FIORENZA
CASIANO FLORISTAN • PAULO FREIRE
CLAUDE GEFFRÉ O.P. • NORBERT GREINACHER
GUSTAVO GUTIÉRREZ • PETER HUIZING S.J.
BAS VAN IERSEL S.M.M. • JEAN-PIERRE JOSSUA O.P.
HANS KÜNG • NICHOLAS LASH
RENÉ LAURENTIN • JOHANNES-BAPTIST METZ
DIETMAR MIETH • JÜRGEN MOLTMANN
ROLAND MURPHY O.CARM. • JACQUES POHIER O.P.
DAVID POWER O.M.I. • KARL RAHNER S.J.
LUIGI SARTORI • EDWARD SCHILLEBEECKX O.P.
DAVID TRACY • KNUT WALF
ANTON WEILER • HARALD WEINRICH
JOHN ZIZIOULAS

"A courageous and timely work. *Concilium* illumines the great
issues of today."
—*America*

"The most ambitious crash program ever undertaken in theological
re-education. The essays are uncompromisingly competent, solid,
and nourishing. *Concilium* is indispensable."
—*The Christian Century*

"A bold and confident venture in contemporary theology. All the
best new theologians are contributing to this collective summa."
—*Commonweal*

THE SEABURY PRESS, NEW YORK   T. & T. CLARK, EDINBURGH

Pig
and
Pug

For Empress Evelyn Pookena Bluebell (a.k.a. Pookie) and for
Sir Francis Bacon (a.k.a. Francey-Pants), and most of all, for Kelley
—L. B.

To my pudgy pigs and muses, Mr. Pickles and Bella
—G. C.

SIMON & SCHUSTER BOOKS FOR YOUNG READERS
An imprint of Simon & Schuster Children's Publishing Division
1230 Avenue of the Americas, New York, New York 10020
Text copyright © 2015 by Lynne Berry
Illustrations copyright © 2015 by Gemma Correll
All rights reserved, including the right of reproduction in whole or in part in any form.
SIMON & SCHUSTER BOOKS FOR YOUNG READERS is a trademark of Simon & Schuster, Inc.
For information about special discounts for bulk purchases, please contact Simon & Schuster
Special Sales at 1-866-506-1949 or business@simonandschuster.com.
The Simon & Schuster Speakers Bureau can bring authors to your live event. For more
information or to book an event, contact the Simon & Schuster Speakers Bureau at
1-866-248-3049 or visit our website at www.simonspeakers.com.
Book design by Lucy Ruth Cummins
The text for this book is hand lettered by the artist.
The illustrations for this book are rendered digitally.
Manufactured in China
0315 SCP
2 4 6 8 10 9 7 5 3 1
CIP data for this book is available from the Library of Congress.
ISBN 978-1-4814-2131-7
ISBN 978-1-4814-2132-4 (eBook)

first edition

Pig
and
Pug

written by

Lynne
Berry

illustrated by

Gemma
Correll

Simon & Schuster
Books for Young Readers
New York   London   Toronto   Sydney   New Delhi

Pug in a purse.

Pug sees Pig.

Pig sees Pug.

Pig hops.
Pug hops.

says Pug.

says Pug.

Pig sees red.

Pig sees black.

Pug pokes Pig.

I will not!

Pig and Pug
pounce.

Pug  chases Pig.

Pig chases Pug.

Pug pants.

Pig snorts.

Pug drops.

Pig flops.

Pug starts to snore.

"Are you asleep?" says Pig to Pug.

Pug grunts.

Pig grunts.

Pug looks at Pig.

Copycat!
says Pug
to Pig.

I am not.
says Pig
to Pug.

Pig sees black.

Pig sees red.

Pug slips and trips and takes a roll—

right into a muddy hole.

Pug sees Pig—
through muddy globs.

Pig winks.
Pug grins.

Pig giggles.
Pug giggles.

Pig pulls Pug from the mud.

(At least for now...)